Annie Bell

# gorgeousdesserts

Annie Bell

# gorgeousdesserts

with photographs by Chris Alack

Kyle Books

This edition published in 2005 by Kyle Books
An imprint of Kyle Cathie Limited
www.kylecathie.com

Distributed by National Book Network
4501 Forbes Blvd., Suite 200
Lanham, MD 20706
Phone: (301) 459 3366  Fax: (301) 429 5746

First published by Kyle Cathie Limited 2005

ISBN 978-1-904920-81-6

The Library of Congress Cataloging-in-Publication Data is available on file.

10 9 8 7 6 5 4 3 2 1

Editor: Stephanie Evans
Design: pinkstripedesign.com
Proofreader: Sharon Brown
Indexer: Ursula Caffrey
Americanizer: Delora Jones
Photographer: Chris Alack
Food Stylists: Lorna Brash, Clare Lewis, Kim Morphew, Penny Stephens
Props Stylist: Sue Radcliffe
Production: Sha Huxtable & Alice Holloway

Color reproduction: Colourscan, Singapore
Printed and bound in Singapore by Star Standard Industries Pty. Ltd.

# contents

# introduction

Some of us could happily live off desserts, and it is only our waistline that makes us see sense. While their role is to round off lunch or dinner, desserts—like cakes or candies—are one of life's trivial indulgences, a treat. And in our house we tend to reserve them for weekends, they are a ritual part of any Saturday and Sunday. Woe betide should I forget or forego something lovely to finish with: I am cajoled by my son who I think must count down from Monday until we get to that sweet treat. Desserts make any occasion seem more special than it might otherwise have been. So much so that to invite friends over for a meal and not go to the trouble of producing some sort of

dessert almost seems rude—it is an accepted part of hospitality. And if it's a real extravaganza, then there is every reason to go to town and dish up several, a grand finale almost like a dessert buffet, and you can guarantee that everyone will insist on trying a little of each one.

## sweet gorgeousness

And, again like cakes, desserts belong firmly in the realm of the home kitchen; they make mothers out of the least domestic of us. It doesn't really matter if you hate ironing, are hopeless with a vacuum, and can't thread a needle to save your life, turn out a winning plum pie and custard and all is forgiven. At least, I like to think so. But more than that I am rarely tempted by the dessert menu in restaurants, as invariably they arrive as overly-contrived dainties, when my idea of a real dessert is something that you can sink into and wallow, a generous splash of sweet gorgeousness.

I mean the kind of desserts that have "forbidden" writ large all over them, which only adds to their allure. Big bowls of steaming fluffy chocolate sponge cake drowned in a salty caramel sauce, a wobbly bread and butter pudding or Sussex pond pudding that spills a lavish buttery lemon sauce from a suet crust. Or a dip down through the layers of a good old English sherry trifle, through that thick bank of syllabub to the fruit and sponge cake soaked in sherry and brandy below. Or a contented foray into a warm rhubarb crumble bubbling with sticky pink juices at the edges.

## when less is more

But desserts don't have to be this indulgent—my love of
jellos grows with every summer season. They're as playful
as they are sharp-witted, relying on that teasing texture.
Choose from a grown-up palate of jellybean flavors,
watermelon, pomegranate, orange, and more exotically
campari and lemon, or blackberry with Earl Grey tea. The
ultimate though is the fashion statement for champagne
jelly, captured bubbles and all that fizzes as you eat it.

Perfectly ripe fruits in season too, afforded the
minimum attention, will leave you feeling sufficiently
virtuous compared to what might have been. A cooling
strawberry soup, fragrant slivers of melon doused with
vodka, juicy black cherries dipped into chocolate
fondue, or figs scattered with amaretti and grilled.

One step up from that are creamy little puddings, a
tingling everlasting lemon syllabub, or a towering
raspberry blancmange, now that Marie Antoinette has
been reinstated as a heroine. And for diehard
traditionalists, a simple flan (crème caramel), with its
glassy golden surface.

And when I haven't had time to make a dessert specially,
then I tend to dip into the freezer for a scoop of
homemade ice cream. This doesn't have to involve a
machine to qualify in the luxury stakes, a dark chocolatey
semifreddo for instance is no more complicated than
making custard. And for those seriously lazy days there
are a handful of easy cheats that rely on a few cartons of
sherbet or ice cream picked up on your way through the
stores, to whip up a striped Neapolitan-style ice, or a
vanilla bombe that spills cherry red jam.

# dressing for dinner

This couldn't be easier; it's not the type of dessert but the accessories that go with it. Ices and syllabubs can be dolled up with delicate dessert cookies—almost anything Italian or French will do. A simple compote with toasted pound cake is divine. And hot desserts relish fancy creams, chantilly, or crème fraîche laced with a little liqueur or eau de vie.

I have a large liqueurs cabinet reserved almost exclusively for making desserts because I love to accentuate and highlight flavors. Cointreau casts a little orange magic, amaretto enlivens almonds, Calvados warms apples, kirsch does it for cherries, a framboise eau de vie lends an accent to raspberries, and Kahlúa brings out the best in coffee. I like to combine summer berries with sweet wines and liqueurs too, berries stacked in a jar with sugar and drowned with rum are a warming excuse to eat with ice cream on a chilly evening. While the strawberries I buy out in Normandy where we have a farmhouse—Marais des Bois and Gariguettes with their intense wild strawberry scent—are just perfect steeped in chilled Sauternes or other sweet wine.

## perfect presentation

Any creamy little puddings, chilled custards, soufflés or mousses and jellos can be made in small coffee cups or glasses. I have a wonderful set of vintage champagne coupes, which have long since relinquished their role of sipping fizz, that make beautiful dishes for such desserts. On a more traditional note, I swear by old-fashioned pudding molds, in fact I have stacks of these in different sizes that multitask in the kitchen.

For English trifles you want a glass bowl, about 3¼ inches deep. I rarely recommend special equipment or serving dishes, but to make a trifle in anything other than a glass bowl is like drawing the curtains when the sun's out. I love to see the way the layers fuse into each other and get acquainted as they go down. Though when you do want them to look dressier than usual, then it's off to the cake decorating supply shop for some bling—shimmering candied flowers or silver dragees.

So choose your dessert and get cooking. This is where I find myself revealing my true colors. There are those who begin with the appetizer and work forwards, and those who begin with the dessert and work backwards....

# fab fruits

These little desserts are simple by design; there's little in the way of dressing up and fancy footwork—the fruits themselves shine through. I tend to place strawberries and cream at the heart of this genre: it's the benchmark that can range from boring to sublime. So elementary, a cliché even, that most people will actually apologize for serving them at the end of a sparkling dinner. But in good shape and in season, there's no point in dishing them up in a more elaborate way, and that goes for any number of other fruits. There's no apology here for popping a few fragrant sun-ripened raspberries into a glass, filling it with chilled champagne, and dishing it up as a dessert. Or, steeping strawberries in Sauternes, if you want to forego the cream.

Pretty much everything else lies in the same vein: the very minimum of fuss to bring out the best in whatever gorgeous fruits you have at hand—provided that they're in season. We've become so accustomed to seeing peaches, plums, and strawberries at Christmas we hardly question their appearance. But they might as well be different fruits altogether, when you compare them to their sweet and juicy summer selves. Better to call on apples and pears in winter, a fluffy chocolate sponge cake, or a bread and butter pudding, and save summer fruits for the treat that they should be.

Some fruits are almost better gently cooked than raw, such as figs, baked with a little almond-scented crumble of amaretti and butter, that relax into something halfway to jam, or plums baked in the oven, which turn lusciously fleshy and dye the sweet and sour syrup a deep purple. But as winter takes hold it's big misshapen Bramley apples that I crave, their cores cut out and filled with dried fruits and spices, which fluff up in the oven and spill out from the skin.

An excuse to finish on a high note, the raspberries cast a little of their magic into the bubbles, and themselves take on something of the wine. Another favorite ruse in this vein is to steep a pound and a half of strawberry halves in half a bottle of chilled Sauternes or Montbazillac for an hour. Do seek out really fragrant fruit varieties for either of these desserts, they're recipes to save for when these fruits are in-season.

# raspberries in champagne

¾ pound raspberries
  (about 2¼–2¾ cups)
½ bottle pink or white champagne,
  chilled

Serves 6

Divide the raspberries between six glasses and pour the champagne over them. First eat the raspberries with a teaspoon, and then drink the champagne.

# rumpot

Rumpot is another way of acquainting ripe summer fruit with alcohol, but you're thinking ahead to cold winter evenings, as rumpot gets better with every month that passes. Then again, if you can't wait, dip in after a couple of days.

½ pound raspberries
  (about 1½ cups)
⅓ cup superfine sugar
¾ cup cherries, pitted
1 cup white rum

Makes 2 cups

Preheat the oven to 375°F. Remove the seal from a 1-pint wide-mouthed hermetic canning jar, put this in the oven for 5 minutes to sterilize then let it cool. Place half the raspberries in the jar and scatter a third of the sugar over them. Layer the cherries on top, scatter another third of the sugar over that, then fill the jar with the remaining raspberries and scatter the last of the sugar on top. The fruit should reach the top of the jar. Pour the rum over the fruit and gently press down on the fruit to submerge it. Slip the rubber seal into place and clip the jar shut. Place in a cool dark place for several months. I turn it several times during the first 24 hours to encourage the sugar to dissolve, and then set it upright an hour or two later. Serve the fruit with ice cream, and you can enjoy the liquor as an after-dinner liqueur.

This is one for the autumn, when blackberries and pears have a brief spell when they're in season together, though as new varieties are developed that season grows ever longer. The rosé dyes pears a pretty shade of pink and gives them a delicious winey flavor, but you could just as well use red wine—that classically renders them a deep Renaissance hue.

# pears in rosé

2½ cups rosé wine

¾ cup superfine sugar

3-inch cinnamon stick

2-inch strip of orange zest,
   removed with a potato peeler

1 bay leaf

6 pears

½ pound blackberries
   (about 1½–2 cups)

**Serves 6**

Place the wine, sugar, cinnamon stick, orange zest, and bay leaf in a medium pan. Bring to a boil, cover, and simmer over a low heat for 15 minutes.

Meanwhile peel the pears. Add them to the pan and cover with a circle of baking parchment (optional) and then the lid. Bring back to a simmer and poach for 15–20 minutes or until tender, turning them over halfway through. Remove them to a bowl. Simmer the remaining syrup until it's reduced by a third and is quite viscous. Pour the syrup over the fruit, leaving in the flavoring ingredients. Once cool, cover and chill for several hours, turning the pears halfway through to ensure they are evenly dyed by the syrup. The pears look beautiful served whole, but if you prefer you can quarter and core them before chilling, again stirring them halfway through.

Bring back up to room temperature for 30 minutes before eating. Remove and discard the flavoring ingredients, and stir in the blackberries.

Iles flottantes or floating islands are divinely moussey poached meringues that melt in the mouth, and they're very French, which is always a recommendation. They often arrive on a pool of almond custard, but their remit goes well beyond that, and I serve them with whatever takes my fancy: in the early summer it's poached cherries. You may like to serve a plate of lacy almond tuiles or other dessert cookies.

# floating islands with cherries

## Cherries

1½ pounds cherries, pitted
    (about 4–5 cups)
¼ cup sugar
4½ tablespoons Calvados or brandy
Squeeze of lemon juice

## Floating islands

2 large egg whites
Pinch of sea salt
¼ cup superfine sugar
Crème fraîche, for serving
    (if unavailable, use sour and/or
    heavy cream)

## Serves 6

Preheat the oven to 375°F. Place the cherries in an ovenproof bowl, sprinkle with the sugar, and pour 3 tablespoons of the Calvados or brandy over them. Cover with foil and cook for 1 hour, stirring them once. Strain the juices into a small saucepan and simmer to reduce by about half until you have a rich syrup. Stir in the remaining brandy and a squeeze of lemon juice, and pour the syrup back over the cherries.

To make the floating islands, which takes about 10 minutes, fill a large frying or sauté pan with water and bring it to a simmer. The water should be no more than at a trembling boil. Beat the egg whites in a bowl with the salt. Once they are risen, gradually sprinkle the sugar over them, beating well with each addition until you have a glossy meringue.

To cook the floating islands, drop heaped tablespoons of the meringue mixture into the water using another spoon to help each one slide off—you should have six in all. Turn them after 30 seconds using a slotted spatula and cook for another 30 seconds. Remove and drain them on paper towels or a clean dish towel. The cherries should still be warm; if you've cooked them in advance, gently reheat them.

To serve, place a meringue in six shallow bowls. Spoon the cherries and syrup around each île flottante, with some crème fraîche in the center.

Here chilled cubes of fragrant ripe melon are macerated in vodka. The idea is to have three different melons and to play on their different characters, and you could also stir in some raspberries before serving. It's thirst-quenching hot-weather fare—a good one for a barbecue—that doubles in quantity with little extra effort and sits chilling in the fridge until you're ready.

# chilled melon medley in vodka

½ cantaloupe melon
   (about 1¼ pounds)
½ honeydew melon
   (about 1¼ pounds)
¼ small watermelon
   (about 1¾ pounds)
1 cup vodka
1½ cups raspberries (optional)

Serves 4–6

Cut the skin off each chunk of melon, taking care to remove the hard outer pale flesh as well. Scoop out the seeds from the cantaloupe and honeydew and cut the fruit into ¾-inch pieces. Cut the watermelon into ¾-inch slices, scoop out any seeds, and then chop it up. Combine the melon in a large bowl, pour the vodka over it, cover, and chill overnight, stirring once or twice.

Just before serving, stir the raspberries, if using, into the chilled melon and scoop into serving bowls, with the juices poured over them.

Nothing challenging here, just a gentle warm milk chocolate cream to dip into, which will have children clamoring for their daily portions of fruit. You can always use orange juice instead of brandy.

# cherries with chocolate fondue

7 ounces good milk chocolate
 (e.g., Lindt), broken into pieces
 (about 1–1¼ cups)
1 tablespoon brandy or dark rum
½ cup light cream
2 pounds cherries

Serves 6

Gently melt the chocolate in the top of a double boiler set over a little simmering water. Add the brandy or rum, and cream, and whisk until smooth. Transfer to a bowl and serve with the cherries alongside to dip into it. The fondue can also be made in advance, in which case let it cool, then cover and chill, and gently rewarm as though melting chocolate.

## hot buttered cherries

I first ate this memorable dessert at the Auberge de Cassagne in Avignon, in Provence, a simple recipe for these beautiful fruits that the chef kindly demonstrated. Melt about ½ cup (1 stick) unsalted butter and ½ cup sugar together in a large frying pan. Once it is seething, add 2 tablespoons kirsch or other fruit eau de vie, and simmer for a minute until the sauce is smooth. Add a pound and a half of cherries and cook for 5 minutes stirring them occasionally, then let them cool for a few minutes. Serve them hot in their syrup with a scoop of vanilla ice cream on top.

This is yummy served with thick slices of toasted Madeira cake or pound cake and clotted or untreated thick cream. Just before serving, preheat the broiler, cut about 6 slices of cake into sticks ¾-inch wide, and lay them out on the rack of a broiler pan. Broil the cake sticks on one side, watching carefully because once they start to color they go very quickly. Turn and dust them with cinnamon and broil the second side, too. You could replace half the red currants with black currants, and use other berries as well as raspberries.

# fruitcage compote

18 ounces red currants
   (about 4¾–5 cups)
¾ cup sugar
1½ pounds raspberries or
   loganberries (about 4½–5½ cups)
Madeira cake or pound cake,
   toasted, for serving (optional)

Serves 6

String the red currants (see page 171) into a small pan using a fork, add the sugar, and gently heat together for 4–5 minutes, stirring occasionally until the fruit is soft but still retains its shape, and is sitting in a pool of syrup. Place half the currants in a fine mesh strainer and press their juice into a bowl and then return it to the pan, discarding the solids. Fold in the other berries, stir well, and heat very gently for a minute or two, not to cook them but to encourage them to release their juices. Transfer the fruit to a serving bowl and let cool. Cover and chill if not serving in the near future, and bring the compote back up to room temperature half an hour before eating.

Don't be deterred by the word soup, this is still 100 percent dessert. It's as cooling as an iced drink—a strawberry puree spiked with Cointreau with a few whole berries. It makes a graceful note on which to end, especially if you dress it up with lavender petals and cigarettes Russe.

# strawberry soup

3 pounds strawberries, hulled
½ cup confectioners' sugar
   (sifted)
4 tablespoons Cointreau
   or Grand Marnier
Squeeze of lemon juice

## For serving
Crème fraîche (or sour and/or
   heavy cream)
Lavender petals (optional)
Toasted brioche or
   cigarettes Russes (optional)

Serves 6

Quarter 2 cups of the strawberries, cover, and chill. Puree the rest in a blender along with the confectioners' sugar, liqueur, and lemon juice. Strain through a fine mesh strainer, taste, and add a little more sifted confectioners' sugar if needed. Cover and chill for a couple of hours.

Divide the strawberry puree between six shallow soup bowls. Place a pile of the reserved strawberries in the center, top with a teaspoon of crème fraîche, then scatter with lavender if you have any, and accompany with toasted brioche or cigarettes Russes, if you like.

Baking figs brings out the best in them: that lovely musky scent and succulence—and here amaretti provide a crispy crumble-like top. This is a genuine quickie: 5 minutes to assemble and 10 minutes to cook.

# amaretti-stuffed figs

9 fresh figs, stalks trimmed,
   and cut in half
3 ounces soft amaretti
2 tablespoons unsalted butter
2½ tablespoons light brown sugar
Crème fraîche or Greek yogurt,
   for serving

**Serves 4**

Preheat the oven to 400°F. Arrange the fig halves cut-side up in a baking dish with a little space in between. Whizz the amaretti, butter, and sugar together in a food processor until the crumbs start to cling together into a crumble. Scatter this over the figs and bake for 10–15 minutes until golden.

To serve, I like them best hot or warm, with crème fraîche or Greek yogurt, though they're still good cold.

## figs with mascarpone and saffron

Another lazy take is to spread about 6 halved figs with mascarpone and broil them. Blend ⅔ cup mascarpone with ¼ cup confectioners' sugar in a bowl, and if you like, add a little saffron liquor made from infusing saffron strands in hot water. Spread the mascarpone mixture over the cut side of each fig half, sprinkle with a little brown sugar, and broil them for 4–5 minutes until golden and bubbling on top.

# roast plums

The plums emerge from the oven in a pool of beautiful sticky deep purple juice, and are particularly good served with a raspberry sherbet. If using sorbet instead of sherbet, remember to allow sorbet 20 minutes at room temperature before serving if it's frozen solid.

12 large juicy red plums,
  stalks removed
¼ cup demerara sugar
4 tablespoons water
3 tablespoons Grand Marnier
  or Cointreau (or water)
Squeeze of lemon juice
2 teaspoons unsalted butter, diced*

## Serves 6

Preheat the oven to 400°F. Place the whole plums in a shallow baking dish that will hold them snugly in a single layer. Scatter the sugar on top and pour the water and Grand Marnier or Cointreau over them. Roast for 25–30 minutes, basting halfway through. Remove the plums to a serving bowl. Sharpen the syrup in the baking dish with a generous squeeze of lemon juice and whisk in the butter. Pour the sauce over the fruit and serve with a spoonful of raspberry sherbet, if you have any.

*The plums are also delicious served at room temperature, in which case omit the butter.

Don't assume that mincemeat means Thanksgiving; it contains everything that apples love—currants, raisins, lots of spices and citrus zest—and it's all there in a jar. You can serve these as they are, or with crème fraîche or clotted or thick cream.

# spicy baked apples

4 Bramley or other large cooking
  apples, each about ½ pound
4 heaping tablespoons mincemeat
4 tablespoons maple syrup
2 tablespoons light brown sugar

**Serves 4**

Preheat the oven to 350°F. Using the tip of a sharp knife, incise a circle around the middle of each apple, to allow them room to expand as they cook without the skin splitting. Cut out a central core from each apple about 1½ inches in diameter. Place the apples in a baking dish that holds them snugly side by side, and loosely stuff the core with the mincemeat. Drizzle the syrup over them, and scatter the sugar on top. Bake for 40–45 minutes, basting them halfway through.

Serve the apples 10–15 minutes out of the oven with the syrupy juices spooned over them.

Luscious poached peaches in a rose-tinted syrup, flecked with black vanilla seeds. But as the recipe title suggests, quality is everything, only worth doing in mid-summer when you can be certain your peaches are dripping with juices.

# peach perfect

6 ripe peaches
scant cup dry white wine
1 vanilla bean, slit
½ cup sugar

## Serves 6

Preheat the oven to 400°F and bring a large pot half filled with water to a boil. Dunk the peaches into the boiling water for 1 minute, then transfer them to a bowl or sink of cold water for another minute or so, and slip off the skins.

Arrange the peaches in a shallow baking dish that holds them snugly, or with just a little space in between, and pour the wine over them. Open out the vanilla bean and scrape out the seeds with a small sharp knife. Blend these with the sugar in a bowl and scatter this over the peaches, then submerge the bean in between the peaches. Cover with foil and bake for 30 minutes, turning the peaches halfway through, and giving the syrup a gentle stir to help the sugar dissolve.

Remove the peaches to a serving dish, pour the syrup over them, leaving in the vanilla bean, and let cool. Cover and chill if not serving in the near future.

jellos

Jellos lie at the ethereal end of the dessert spectrum. Sparkling guilt-free gems, a playful palate-cleansing end to any feast. And after years of being relegated to children's parties, they seem finally to be re-entering the adult arena of appreciation. They lend themselves to flavors as intense as their vibrant colors, in line with fruit pastilles or wine gums—strawberry, orange, and blackberry—and those we can only wish for like pomegranate and watermelon. Almost anything else we prize by the small cup or glass is just as game: freshly brewed black coffee, rust-hued rooibos tea, and, the ultimate, champagne or Prosecco—captured bubbles and all. If it tastes good to drink, then just think how delicious it'll taste once it's set.

The availability of leaf gelatin (see page 47) has made homemade jellos more accessible. Once the sole preserve of chefs, leaf gelatin makes life very much easier; a mere glance at boiling water or liquid and it melts instantly. Granulated gelatin is a good second best, but steering it towards being fully dissolved is more challenging. It was a long time before I discovered the secret: to gently heat it in a small bowl or top of a double boiler set over a pan with a little simmering water in it as though melting chocolate. Dissolved this way there's no chance of it boiling, which is ruination to any set. But the texture is something you can play around with; be guided but not ruled by the package instructions—you may prefer a light, almost creamy set that dissolves the minute you start eating it, or a firmer one if you are planning on turning out the jellos or using them as a showcase for other delights.

It's in the nature of a jello to thrill, not least with its texture, but its appearance, too. Setting fruits and other goodies into jello is a trip back to the craft of making resin molds. Instead of shells, leaves, stones, and other such treasures, it's hidden fruits. The trick here is to let your jello set in the fridge for about two hours, by which time it will have gelled enough to support any fruit you put into it without sinking. They're probably the prettiest of all desserts, too, either turned out or made in little glass bowls or dishes; there seems little point in hiding their light under a bushel.

Capturing bubbles in jello is a party trick that makes a great finale; the fizz is an amuse bouche in the true definition of the phrase, and creates a texture quite unlike any other jello—almost crumbly. There's no need for anything on the side, except perhaps a few chocolates to offset all that virtue, and some coffee to follow.

# saffron and prosecco jello

7 gelatin leaves, cut into broad strips
   (or 2¼ envelopes granulated gelatin,
   see page 47)
1 bottle Prosecco, chilled
¾ cup superfine sugar
About 20 saffron filaments, ground

**Serves 6**

Place a 1-quart glass bowl (or six champagne flutes if you have room) in the freezer for several hours or overnight. Place the gelatin strips in a bowl, cover with cold water, and let soak for 5 minutes, then drain. Bring ½ cup of the Prosecco to a boil in a small pan with the sugar, stirring until it dissolves. Pour this over the saffron and blend, and then over the gelatin, again stirring until it dissolves.

Pour the gelatin solution into the chilled bowl, then gradually pour the rest of the bottle of Prosecco over it, constantly stirring to combine it with the gelatin. Spoon off any foam. Return the bowl to the freezer for 1 hour, then place it in the fridge for several hours longer or overnight until set.

A sparkling ruby red jello, courtesy of a carton of juice that whisks you to the finishing line in minutes. This is a good one at any time of year, but dwell on it especially around Christmas, when pondering on a way of weaving these fruits into your celebrations.

# pomegranate jello

6 gelatin leaves, cut into
    broad strips (or 2 envelopes
    granulated gelatin, see
    page 47)
½ cup strawberry jam
2½ cups pomegranate juice
Juice of ½ lemon
1 pomegranate, cut in half
Rose petals, for decoration
    (optional)

### Rose cream (optional)

1¼ cups whipping cream
½ cup confectioners' sugar, sifted
2 teaspoons rosewater

### Serves 6

Place the gelatin strips in a bowl, cover with cold water, and let soak for 5 minutes, then drain.

Gently heat the jam in a small saucepan until it softens, mashing it with a spoon, then blend in a little of the pomegranate juice. Add the remaining juice, and the lemon juice, and heat until the liquid feels warm to the touch.

Pour a little of the juice over the soaked gelatin and stir until it dissolves. Stir the gelatin solution back into the juice and strain it through a fine mesh strainer into a serving bowl—it looks especially pretty in a glass one. Cover and chill overnight.

To serve, free the pomegranate seeds by pressing down on the skin to pop them out, then pick out and discard any white pith. Serve the seeds scattered over the jello and decorate with rose petals, if using.

To make the rose cream, whisk the whipping cream, sugar, and rosewater in a bowl until it forms soft, fluffy peaks; I use an electric beater. Cover and chill until needed. If leaving it longer than a couple of hours, give it a stir and gently whisk with a spoon before serving with the jello.

If you ever reach the point when you feel utterly replete after a lovely meal with friends, and the idea of getting up to make coffee casts a shadow over your peace but you feel the need to do the honorable, here is one way of circumventing the dilemma, and as it takes in dessert too, you should be left feeling doubly relaxed.

# black with cream

4 gelatin leaves, cut into broad strips
  (or 1⅓ envelopes granulated gelatin,
  see page 47)
2½ cups freshly brewed coffee
½ cup sugar
2 tablespoons crème fraîche (or heavy
  cream)
Chocolate powder, for dusting

Place the gelatin strips in a bowl, cover with cold water, and let soak for 5 minutes, then drain.

Pour the coffee over the sugar in a measuring cup or bowl and stir until it dissolves. Pour about half of this onto the soaked gelatin and stir until it melts, then stir the solution back into the coffee. Divide the solution between six small coffee cups or ⅔-cup ramekins. Let cool, then cover and chill overnight until set (I put them in a roasting dish first to keep them from tipping over). Serve the jellos with a teaspoon of crème fraîche and a dusting of chocolate powder.

As a child I longed to try watermelon after watching Goofy munching on a slice and spitting out the seeds like a stream of gunfire. But I was disappointed when I got there, was the texture really worth all that trouble? Well, they've made life that much easier for today's children with the near absence of obvious seeds in the majority of varieties, but that still leaves the texture, and a cool rose-pink jello has to be the answer.

# watermelon jello

6 gelatin leaves, cut into broad strips
  (or 2 envelopes granulated gelatin,
  see page 47)
2 pounds watermelon flesh (trimmed
  weight), cubed, large seeds removed
2 tablespoons lemon juice
¾ cup sugar
1¼ cups whipping cream, whipped
1 ounce shelled pistachios, finely
  chopped or ground in a food
  processor (about ⅓ cup)

**Serves 6**

Place the gelatin strips in a bowl, cover with cold water, and let soak for 5 minutes, then drain.

Place the watermelon in a blender and reduce to a puree. Press it through a fine mesh strainer into a 1-quart measuring cup, and add the lemon juice. You should have about 3⅓ cups of liquid. Transfer this to a small saucepan and heat gently with the sugar until this dissolves; it should feel hot if you dip in your finger, without scalding. Add the soaked gelatin and stir until it dissolves.

Pour the solution into a glass serving dish (about 8 inches across x 3 inches deep), or six individual ones, let cool, then cover and chill for 2 hours until the jello has just started to set. Give it a stir, then cover and chill overnight.

Shortly before serving, place a spoonful of whipped cream on the jello and scatter the pistachios over it.

The "really orange" is an intense hit of the fruit. It reminds me of that wonderful frozen orange juice concentrate that was the last word in luxury in England during my childhood. It came in cans and if you diluted it with a can of water, it tasted just like sorbet if you managed to get in there when your mother wasn't looking. The chocolate custard is for chocolate-orange fiends, and is actually rather good on its own.

# really orange jello

### Jello

3 x 6-ounce cans frozen orange
   juice concentrate
8 gelatin leaves, cut into broad strips
   (or 2⅔ envelopes granulated
   gelatin, see page 47)
2 oranges
miniature chocolate orange segments
   or grated chocolate (optional)

### Chocolate custard

1¾ cups milk
4 medium organic egg yolks
3 ounces milk chocolate (e.g., Lindt),
   broken into pieces (about ½ cup)
5 ounces dark chocolate (50%
   cocoa), broken into pieces
   (about ¾–1 cup)

### Serves 6

Defrost the concentrate entirely, then combine with 2¾ cups water until thoroughly blended.

Place the gelatin strips in a bowl, cover with cold water, and let soak for 5 minutes, then drain. Pour a little of the concentrate orange juice over the gelatin and stir until it dissolves, then add this back to the rest of the orange juice. Pour into a glass serving bowl.

Cut the skin and pith off the oranges, and run a sharp knife between the segments to remove them. Scatter these over the surface of the jello—they should float. Cover and chill overnight. Serve the jello with the chocolate custard on top, and if you like, a chocolate orange segment or two. The jello can be made several days in advance, in which case you can reduce the amount of gelatin to 6 leaves, as it will continue to set over a period of time.

To make the chocolate custard, break the egg yolks into a bowl. Bring the milk to a boil, whisk it into the egg yolks, then strain it through a fine mesh strainer into a bowl. At the same time, gently melt all the chocolate in the top of a double boiler over a little simmering water. Whisk in the egg custard, in four goes, until you have a rich chocolate cream. Cover and let cool, then chill for several hours or overnight.

I'm always on the lookout for ways of serving summer fruits beyond their usual remit of "with cream," gorgeous though that is. This recipe has a clean and light edge, with the rasping hint of a little syrupy white wine in the way of gentle vice. The call for pretty small glass dishes or champagne coupes is greater than ever.

# summer jello

3 gelatin leaves, cut into broad
   strips (or 1 envelope granulated
   gelatin, see page 47)
2½ cups Sauternes, or other
   sweet white wine
1½ tablespoons sugar
1 cup strawberries
⅓ cup blueberries
⅓ cup raspberries

### Serves 4

Place the gelatin strips in a bowl, cover with cold water, and let soak for 5 minutes, then drain.

Bring the wine and sugar to a boil in a small pan, then immediately remove from the heat. Pour 3–4 tablespoons of the hot wine over the soaked gelatin and stir to dissolve, then add this back to the wine. Pour into four small glass bowls or glasses (allowing room for the addition of fruit), or into one large one. Cool, and then chill for 2–3 hours until the jello is starting to set.

Hull the strawberries and cut in half if they are large. Fold all the fruit into the jello, cover, and let set overnight in the fridge.

# whisked wine jello

4 gelatin leaves, cut into broad strips
   (or 1⅓ envelopes granulated gelatin,
   see page 47)
1 bottle Sauternes or other sweet
   white wine
about 4 tablespoons superfine sugar,
   or to taste
fruits of your choice, to spoon the
   jello over

### Serves 4–6

Place the gelatin strips in a bowl, cover with cold water, and let soak for 5 minutes, then drain. Bring the wine to a boil in a pan and simmer for a couple of minutes, then remove from the heat. Add the sugar to taste, depending on the sweetness of the wine—your jello should be sweeter than you might want to drink, to counter the acidity of whatever fruits you'll be spooning it over. Pour a little heated wine over the gelatin and stir until it dissolves, then add this back to the wine solution. Pour into a bowl and let cool, then cover and chill for 6 hours or overnight until it has set. To serve, run a whisk through it to break it up into a soft chopped mass and spoon it over whatever fruits you are serving (choose from pitted cherries, sliced peaches, raspberries, loganberries, and strawberries).

When Jo Malone launched her wonderful esoteric perfume range, it was an inspiration in how scents were created. The way she subtly employed fruits and spices to lift other notes was the starting point for this jello, as mysterious as it is dark. A prize for anyone who guesses the tea that so naturally flows as an undercurrent to the blackberry.

# blackberry and tea jello

3 gelatin leaves, cut into broad strips (or 1 envelope
  granulated gelatin, see page 47)
⅓ cup sugar
1¾ cups hot Earl Grey tea
¾ pound blackberries (about 2½–3 cups)
Silver balls (optional)

## Serves 6

Place the gelatin strips in a bowl, cover with cold water, and let soak for 5 minutes, then drain.

Add the sugar to the hot tea in a measuring cup or bowl and stir until it dissolves. Pour about half of this onto the soaked gelatin and stir until it melts, then stir the solution back into the tea. Set aside 6 juicy blackberries for decoration, and puree the rest in a blender. Strain the puree through a fine mesh strainer, and stir it into the tea. Pour the solution into six ⅔-cup ramekins or small glasses. Let cool, then cover and chill overnight until set (I put them in a roasting dish first to keep them from tipping over).

Serve each jello with a blackberry in the center and a few silver balls for added glitz, if you like.

Also known as Red Bush, we have latched on to this rust-colored tea that grows wild in South Africa, not least because it sings with anti-oxidants and has the greatest anti-aging properties of any plant in the world. You can't ask much more than that from a dessert.

# rooibos jello

3 gelatin leaves, cut into broad strips
  (or 1 envelope granulated gelatin,
  see page 47)
⅔ cup sugar
3 tablespoons rooibos tea
Juice of 1 orange
1 tablespoon lemon juice
2 passionfruit, cut in half

Serves 4

Place the gelatin strips in a bowl, cover with cold water, and let soak for 5 minutes, then drain.

Place the sugar in a measuring cup, fill up to the 2-cup mark with boiling water and stir to dissolve. Pour this over the tea in another measuring cup or in a teapot, give it a stir, and let it infuse for 5 minutes. Strain the tea through a fine-mesh strainer or tea-strainer over the gelatin and stir to dissolve. Add the orange and lemon juice and strain through a strainer a second time, into a measuring cup or bowl.

Rinse four ⅔-cup ramekins or small glasses or molds. Pour the jello solution into them and let cool. Cover with plastic wrap (I put them in a roasting dish first to keep from tipping over), then place in the fridge to set overnight.

To serve, either smooth the passionfruit seeds over the top of each dish of jello, or briefly dip the molds into a bowl of boiling water, run a knife around the edge, and turn out onto plates. Spoon the seeds over and around them.

This is kiddie heaven, something like a glorious fruit pastille that's a bit bigger than usual.

# strawberry jellos

3 gelatin leaves, cut into broad strips
   (or 1 envelope granulated gelatin,
   see page 47)
2 pounds strawberries
½ cup sugar
Juice of 1 lemon
Clotted or heavy cream (optional)

## Serves 4

Place the gelatin strips in a bowl, cover with cold water, and soak for 5 minutes, then drain.

Set aside 4 small strawberries for decoration and hull the rest, cutting up large ones. Puree these in a blender with the sugar and lemon juice, then strain the puree through a fine mesh strainer into a small pan. Bring to a boil, then pour it into a measuring cup, you should have about 2½ cups of liquid (make up the amount with water if need be).

Pour a little of this over the soaked gelatin and stir to dissolve, then stir in the rest. Divide the jello solution between four ⅔-cup ramekins or other little molds and let cool. Cover and chill overnight. Serve decorated with a strawberry in the middle, and a spoon of clotted cream, if you like.

Campari with lemon is an acquired taste for those with a penchant for a little sophisticated bitterness in their life, but try this jello and it's easy to see why they're thrown together: good friends that reveal each other's hidden charms.

# campari and lemon jellos with passionfruit

4 gelatin leaves, cut into
broad strips (or 1⅓
envelopes granulated
gelatin, see page 47)
¾ cup sugar
Juice of 3 lemons

2 tablespoons Campari
3 passionfruit, cut in half

Serves 6

Place the gelatin strips in a bowl, cover with cold water, and let soak for 5 minutes, then drain.

Place the sugar in a measuring cup and fill up to the 1¼-cups mark with boiling water and stir to dissolve. Pour a little of this over the gelatin and stir to dissolve, then add the gelatin mixture back into the measuring cup. Now add the lemon juice and the Campari and make up to 2½ cups with boiling water. Strain through a fine mesh strainer into six rinsed ⅔-cup ramekins or other little molds. Cover with plastic wrap (I place them in a roasting dish for this and to keep them from tipping over), let cool and then place in the fridge to set overnight.

To serve, briefly dip the molds into a bowl of boiling water, run a knife around the edge, and turn out onto plates. Spoon the seeds from half a passionfruit over each one.

# gelatin

## the set

The amount of gelatin used can be varied depending upon the type of set you want. If you are planning on turning the jello out from a mold, add a little bit extra. Equally, if you like your jello on the wobbly side you can use a little less. It's always worth bearing in mind that the jello will continue to set over a period of days, so if you are making it well in advance, then you can reduce the quantity slightly.

## leaf gelatin

Leaf gelatin dissolves more readily than granulated. However, brands do tend to differ, and not all of them give accurate recommendations for quantities. All these jellos have been tested using Supercook leaf gelatin (a British brand), 4 leaves will set 2½ cups liquid.

To use the leaf form, cut the gelatin into broad strips, place in a bowl, cover with cold water and let soak for 5 minutes, then drain it.

## granulated gelatin

In England, this comes in envelopes of a standard weight of 12g that sets 2½ cups liquid, and I can depend on the Supercook brand to do this reliably. Sprinkle the gelatin over a few tablespoons of just-boiled water in a small bowl, as opposed to the other way around. Leave it for 3–4 minutes to soften, then stir for a minute or two, by which time you should have a clear sticky solution. In the US, granulated gelatin comes in ¼-ounce (7g) envelopes which will set 2 cups of liquid. The recipes in this book have been adjusted to suit the American-sized packets of granulated gelatin.

## problem solving

If the gelatin hasn't completely dissolved, place the bowl within another bowl of just-boiled water and leave it for a few minutes longer, then give it a good stir. Alternatively, pour the mixture into the top of a double boiler or a bowl set over a pan with a little simmering water in it, as though you were melting chocolate, and gently heat. **It's essential the gelatin solution is never actually boiled**, as this will destroy its ability to set.

## adding the gelatin

Ideally add the gelatin solution to a warm base, diluting the molten gelatin with a little warmed liquid first. You can then incorporate it with the rest of the warm jello base.

If you add gelatin solution to a cold liquid it will immediately set into rubbery lumps. There is a way around this, however. If the flavored liquid for the jello is cold, very gradually whisk the cold liquid into the gelatin solution, or add about 8 tablespoons of the cold liquid, one at a time to the gelatin solution, and then add this back to the flavored liquid.

ice cool

This chapter is welcome to everyone, with or without an ice cream maker. You can easily make delectable frozen desserts in their absence that will top anything made in a machine. And with the help of a food processor, you again don't need one. If you half-freeze a mixture, whizz it to a slush, and then continue to freeze it, you will still produce a fine homemade ice cream. And if this seems like too much work, you can have some fun running up wildly extravagant ice cream bombes and layered terrines using tubs of ready-made ice cream and a few other bits and pieces. Let your mind wander to that small square in Italy where you sheltered from the midday sun (or NYC's Little Italy, where you wilted in the city's heat) and chose ices off a picture menu...

I cannot resist the great classic ice creams: a really dense fudgey chocolate or a silky vanilla flecked with the black of vanilla seeds that can be conjured into a Peach Melba with raspberry sauce and slivers of peach, and of course that English eccentric: brown bread ice cream–a mass of caramelized breadcrumbs folded into cream and frozen.  But when I'm after something truly simple, then it's a shot of bitter espresso coffee poured over a scoop of vanilla.

I sometimes favor sorbets or sherbets over ice creams at the end of dinner as they round off an occasion in more palate-cleansing fashion, providing the same sparkle as fresh jellos and fruit. For me, sorbets flavored with deep-hued juices like strawberry and black currant hit the spot: there's something irresistible about a mass of miniscule dark vermilion ice crystals that dye your tongue and lips red or dramatically purple. And while they're delicious eaten within a few hours of being churned, they can also be revived after a week or so–unlike ice creams. Simply let them melt, then add a little hooch or some other conceit should the flavor need enlivening and rechurn the mixture.

The gin makes a nice jazzy touch, and calls up hidden memories of English gardens and lunches. But if you're making this with kiddies in mind, nothing will seem amiss should you omit the gin, and they might appreciate some iced gems scattered over the top.

# strawberry and gin sherbet

1 cup boiling water
1¼ cups sugar
1¾ pounds strawberries, hulled
Juice of 1 lemon
4 tablespoons gin
Cones, for serving

**Serves 8**

Pour the boiling water over the sugar in a bowl, stir until it dissolves and let it cool. Puree the strawberries, lemon juice, and gin in a blender and strain through a fine mesh strainer. Combine the strawberry puree with the syrup, and freeze according to the instructions for your ice cream maker. It is less stressful on the motor if you chill the solution first. Scoop the sherbet into a container, seal, and freeze for several hours or overnight.

Alternatively, pour the mixture into a plastic container, seal it, and freeze for 2–3 hours until it is half-frozen, hard around the outside and soft within, but start checking it after 1 hour. Scoop it into a food processor and whizz to break up the ice crystals, at which point it will be like a thick slush. Return it to the container and freeze for another 2 hours until you have a soft but firm sherbet. If leaving it longer than this and it has frozen solid, it may need 15–30 minutes out of the freezer to return to the right consistency.

Serve in cones to go.

This one takes the title ice cream rather literally, consisting quite simply of crushed raspberries, clotted cream, and confectioners' sugar, chilled down and down. It's designed to be eaten as soon as it's churned, or at least within an hour of being frozen.

# raspberry and clotted cream ice cream

1 pound raspberries (about 3 cups)
1½ cups clotted cream (if unavailable, use heavy cream)
1 cup confectioners' sugar, sifted
Cantuccini, for serving (optional)

### Serves 6

Place the raspberries in the bowl of a food processor and briefly whizz to reduce to a textured puree. Beat the cream and sugar in a large bowl until smooth, then fold in the raspberries in two goes. You can make this in advance and freeze it shortly before serving, in which case cover and chill it at this stage.

Freeze the raspberries and cream mixture according to the instructions for your ice cream maker. Ideally serve the ice immediately, but it will keep in the fridge for up to an hour. Serve with cantuccini, if you like.

This black currant sherbet is the most intensely flavored ice I know, matched by its Renaissance hue of deep purple. In essence it's everything you love about a Kir Royale, in a sophisticated ice cream parlor fashion.

# kir float

18 ounces black currants (about
   5 cups), fresh, or frozen
   and defrosted
¾ cup sugar
⅔ cup water
1 bottle chilled champagne

Serves 6

Place the black currants in a medium pan with the sugar and water. Bring to a boil, then cover and cook over a low heat for 5 minutes. Press the mixture through a fine mesh strainer over a bowl to collect the thick deep-purple syrup. Let this cool, then cover and chill for a couple of hours.

If you have an ice cream maker, then freeze according to the instructions. Scoop the sherbet into a container, seal, and freeze for at least 4 hours or overnight.

Alternatively, transfer the mixture to a shallow container, cover or seal it, and freeze for about 2 hours until the mixture is half-frozen, hard around the outside and soft within, but start checking it after 1 hour. Scoop it into a food processor and whizz to a thick slush to break up the ice crystals. Return the sherbet to the container and freeze for another 4 hours or overnight.

Depending upon how hard the sherbet has frozen, it may need about 20 minutes out of the freezer. Place a scoop of sherbet in the bottom of six glasses and fill up with champagne.

If you had to have just one classic on the menu, a promise of instant cooling palate-cleansing refreshment, then this would have to be it. And OK, you can scoop out some lemons and fill them.

# lemon sherbet

1½ cups boiling water
1¼ cups sugar (refined)
5 lemons

**Serves 4**

Pour the boiling water over the sugar in a bowl and stir until dissolved. Remove the zest from 3 of the lemons using a potato peeler, add to the syrup, and let cool completely for about an hour. Add the juice from the lemons to the syrup, and strain through a fine mesh strainer. Cover and chill the solution for several hours or overnight.

If using an ice cream maker, freeze according to the instructions, then scoop the sherbet into a container or into lemon shells, seal, and freeze for several hours or overnight.

Alternatively pour the solution into a container, seal, and freeze until softly frozen, start checking it after about 3 hours, and hourly thereafter. Scoop the sherbet into the bowl of a food processor and whizz to a slush, then return it to the freezer (or scoop into lemon shells) for another few hours or overnight.

If the sherbet has frozen very hard, then you may need to remove it about 20 minutes before serving.

Every cook needs a really good, rich chocolate ice cream up their sleeve, and this one challenges Häagen-Dazs® for supremacy, who famously set theirs with chocolate chips, which might be worth trying, too.

# really chocolatey semifreddo

3½ ounces dark chocolate
   (70% cocoa), broken into pieces
   (about ½ cup)
1¼ cups heavy cream
3 organic eggs, separated
1 cup confectioners' sugar (sifted)
½ teaspoon vanilla extract
white chocolate shavings, for serving

**Serves 6**

Gently melt the chocolate in the top of a double boiler set over a pan with a little simmering water in it. In a small nonstick pan, bring the cream to a boil. Whisk the egg yolks and half of the sugar together in a bowl, then gradually whisk in the hot cream, it should thicken into a thin custard instantly. Strain it through a fine mesh strainer into a bowl, then whisk it into the melted chocolate in about three goes, and stir in the vanilla. Cover the surface with plastic wrap and let cool to room temperature.

Beat the egg whites until stiff, then gradually sprinkle the remaining sugar over them, a tablespoon at a time, beating well with each addition until you have a stiff glossy meringue; I use a hand-held electric beater. Fold the egg whites into the cooled chocolate custard in two goes. Line a 1½-quart bowl with plastic wrap and pour in the mixture, then cover the surface with plastic wrap and freeze overnight. The ice cream can also be made in a plastic container.

If making it in a bowl as a bombe, dip the bowl into a sink of hot water to loosen the ice cream, then turn it out onto a plate and remove the plastic wrap. Let it soften for about 10 minutes, then scatter with chocolate shavings. Otherwise remove from the freezer about 20 minutes before eating, and serve in scoops with the chocolate shavings scattered over it.

As a child I wanted to emigrate to America, the land where you get marshmallows in cereal, so this version of brown bread ice cream has a certain trans-Atlantic appeal for me. Though the marshmallows aren't essential.

# brown bread and marshmallow ice cream

2½ ounces fresh brown breadcrumbs (about 1½ cups)
⅓ cup light brown sugar
3 medium organic egg whites
⅓ cup confectioners' sugar, sifted

1¼ cups heavy cream
2½ cups mini marshmallows

Serves 6–8

Preheat the oven to 400°F. Whizz together the breadcrumbs and brown sugar in the bowl of a food processor, then spread the mixture out in a thin layer on a baking tray. Toast for 6–8 minutes until the crumbs near the edges of the pan are turning golden. Scrape them into the middle of the pan and spread them out again, and toast for another 2–3 minutes until evenly gold, then let cool for a few minutes.

Beat the egg whites until they have risen, then sprinkle the confectioners' sugar over them, a tablespoon at a time, beating well with each addition, until you have a stiff glossy meringue. In a separate bowl, whip the cream to stiff peaks.

Run a rolling pin over the crumbs to break them up. Fold the egg whites into the cream, then the crumbs and the marshmallows. Transfer the mixture to a container, seal, and freeze overnight. Remove 20–25 minutes before eating.

The plan here is to pour scalding bitter espresso over a scoop of frozen solid vanilla ice cream, then start to work the coffee into the melted edges and eat it spoon by spoon as it softens to a creamy tan-colored ice cream. Like the Black with Cream on page 35, it's one of those desserts that rounds off a delicious lunch or dinner when you feel like something sweet without going the whole hog of a rich dessert.

# affogato al caffe

4 scoops vanilla ice cream, frozen solid

4 shots of freshly brewed espresso coffee

## Serves 4

Whereas normally you need to soften ice cream right from the freezer before serving it, here it should be frozen rock hard. If you are using homemade ice cream (see page 60), churn and freeze it overnight.

Place four scoops of ice cream in four small bowls or cups. Trickle a shot of freshly brewed espresso over each one and serve.

It's those cherry red lips and buttermilk skin that call up this bombe's namesake. This is the easiest possible dessert, you simply have to attend to it in stages, but even then if you forget and leave it in the freezer longer than the specified time, it won't come to any harm.

# snow white bombe

2 x 1-pint tubs vanilla ice cream
½ cup black cherry jam
   (e.g., St. Dalfour)
1½ tablespoons brandy
Generous squeeze of lemon juice
Amaretti, for serving (optional)

## Serves 6

Remove one of the tubs of ice cream from the freezer and let it soften for about 20 minutes. Scoop this into a 1-quart bowl or other similar deep dish, and evenly spread it to line the bottom and sides of the dish. Cover the surface with plastic wrap and freeze for 2 hours until it firms up.

Work the jam in a bowl to loosen it, then blend in the brandy and lemon juice. Fill the cavity of the ice cream bombe—you may have to excavate the hollow again if it has filled itself in. Cover and freeze for another couple of hours.

Remove the second tub of ice cream from the freezer, again let it soften for about 20 minutes, and then fill the bowl to the top and smooth the surface (you will have a little left over in the tub). Cover and freeze overnight.

Remove from the freezer about 20 minutes before serving. Dip the bowl into a sink of hot water, then run a knife around the edge of the bombe and turn it out onto a plate. Serve in slices, with some amaretti if you like.

This is a Sixties-Seventies thing—you may or may not remember those blocks of layered ice cream; perhaps you were too young. This ice cream cake has the hidden surprise of a layer of meringue and jam in the middle. Any summery flavor can be partnered with the chocolate: raspberry, strawberry, peach, cherry ... whatever other delightful hot-weather flavors the freezer cabinet is offering up. Pistachio is particularly good if you can get it.

# neo-politan pavlova ice cream

1 x 1-pint tub chocolate ice cream

1 x 1-pint tub pistachio or other ice cream of contrasting color

⅓ cup raspberry or strawberry jam

3 meringue nests, finely crumbled

## Serves 8

Remove the chocolate ice cream from the freezer 30–45 minutes in advance, so that it's really soft. Smooth the chocolate ice cream over the bottom of an 8½-inch loaf pan, pressing it into the corners and leveling the surface. Wipe any smudges around the edge with paper towels, then cover the surface with plastic wrap and freeze for a couple of hours.

Remove the pistachio ice cream from the freezer 30–45 minutes in advance. Gently heat the jam in a small pan until it loosens, then press it through a strainer to remove the seeds. It should be at room temperature when you use it so let it cool first. Smooth a third of the pistachio ice cream over the chocolate ice cream, scatter the crumbled meringue over it and gently press it down, drizzle the jam over that, then smooth the rest of the ice cream over the top, again pressing it down and smoothing it. Cover the surface with plastic wrap and freeze for at least 4 hours, or overnight.

To serve, briefly dip the loaf pan in a sink of hot water, run a knife around the edge, turn it out onto a plate or board, and cut into slices.

If you were an actress trying to pile on the pounds for a new part, sitting around dipping into a tub of ice cream would do the trick in no time at all. Which, given how close it is to a girl's heart, makes it something of a problem. The Indians seem to have got it just right with kulfi, not as austere as a sherbet, it relies on milk that is reduced to enrich it.

# pistachio kulfi

½ gallon whole milk
1 level teaspoon cornstarch
¾ cup sugar
1 tablespoon rosewater
½ cup shelled pistachios,

### Serves 6

Pour the milk into a large pan, bring to a boil, and simmer for about 45 minutes over a medium heat to reduce by half. Don't worry about the skin that forms during the process of cooking, simply lift this off at the end. Blend 1 tablespoon of the reduced milk with the cornstarch, return it to the saucepan, and simmer for several minutes until it thickens a little. Remove from the heat, add the sugar and stir to dissolve, then add the rosewater. Pour through a strainer into a 1-quart measuring cup or bowl, cover the surface with plastic wrap and let cool. Chill for a couple of hours or overnight.

Grind two thirds of the pistachios to a powder in an electric coffee grinder and finely chop the rest. Stir the ground pistachios into the ice cream mixture, and then stir in the chopped ones.

Freeze the mixture according to the instructions for your ice cream maker. Either serve it immediately, or transfer it to a plastic container, cover, and freeze. It is at its best eaten within about 3 hours, if keeping it any longer then remove from the freezer 30 minutes before serving to allow it to soften a little.

Alternatively pour the solution into a container, seal, and freeze until softly frozen, start checking it after about 2 hours, and hourly thereafter. Scoop the ice into the bowl of a food processor and whizz to a slush, then return it to the freezer for another few hours.

These little cakes are delicious eaten with ice creams and sherbets (or a fruit dessert, see page 13). You can either make them in boat or scallop shapes if your cake-pan cupboard runs to these, or little cupcake molds—your muffin pans will double for these.

# golden raisin madeleines

2 large eggs

2 tablespoons sugar

Finely grated zest of 1 lemon

2 tablespoons clear honey

6 tablespoons all-purpose flour

1 teaspoon baking powder

½ cup ground almonds

½ cup plus 1 tablespoon (1⅛ sticks)
   unsalted butter, melted

⅓ cup golden raisins

Confectioners' sugar, for dusting

## Makes 12–15

Whisk the eggs and sugar together in a bowl until they are almost white. Add the lemon zest and the honey. Sift the flour and baking powder together into a bowl, then lightly fold into the honey mixture with the ground almonds. Brush the insides of the cake pan molds with a little of the melted butter, and fold the rest into the cake batter. Cover and chill the batter for 30 minutes.

Meanwhile, preheat the oven to 400°F. Fold the raisins into the batter and fill the molds by two thirds. Bake for 9–10 minutes until golden.

Run a knife around the edge of the cakes to loosen them and turn them out onto a wire rack to cool. Dust with confectioners' sugar at the last minute and arrange on a plate. While they are nicest eaten barely cooled, you can store them in an airtight container for a couple of days.

This is a classic sugar syrup that can be used for sorbets and sherbets, and poaching fruits or sweetening fruit sauces. It keeps well in the fridge for up to 2 weeks.

# sugar syrup

1½ cups sugar
1½ cups boiling water

## Makes 1¾ cups

Place the sugar in a bowl, pour the boiling water over it, and stir until the sugar dissolves. Let the syrup cool to room temperature, then cover and chill it until required.

It's worth remembering to chill your sherbet mixture before churning to save overworking your ice cream maker, as some of them are more efficient than others.

## the perfect consistency

Most homemade ice cream needs to be removed from the freezer a little bit in advance to ensure it has that soft melting consistency. But how long will depend on the type of ice cream and whether it's resided in an ice-box at the top of the fridge or in a deep-freeze. A quick prod should tell you more or less how long it needs. For just that little bit of softening, then 10–15 minutes should do it; if it's rock hard, then closer to 30 minutes before serving.

# something creamy

Given our historic love of ice cream, it's not hard to see why that extends to other creamy silken desserts, especially when they come in little ceramic cups or glasses. I wonder if we don't sometimes try to fool ourselves that these miniatures are mere will-o'-the-wisps, hardly even counting as dessert. So small in fact, many of us find room for another, and another little cupful of something creamy.

Top prize has to be a competition between crème brûlée and crème caramel (flan), though increasingly my vote goes to the latter, cooling and lightly set, its glassy surface dyed gold with caramel that dissolves into a sauce around it. And it's foolproof, the caramel is guaranteed, unlike a crème brûlée. Mainly due to a reluctance to own a mini blowtorch, I usually try to find other ways of finishing off this delectable cream, whether it's with a jammy fruit compote spread on top, or by flavoring the cream with coffee and scattering some grated chocolate over it.

Fluffy creamy fruit fools also lie close to our heart, anything tart and intense is game, rhubarb makes a particularly spendid fool, and raspberries too are as sour as they are sweet, and that allows for the introduction of lots of cream. Any untreated creams will have that much more to offer than a pasteurized cream so, if available, aim for a nice thick and yellow cream.

But if ever we needed proof that what goes around comes around, and that all food fashions of value reappear at some point, then we have only to look to the recent reinstatement of Marie Antoinette as a French national heroine, and with it the makeover of blancmange. Finally rescued from a corner of the nursery and reborn as deliciously decadent and sexy. Towering pastel-hued custards, an acquired taste perhaps, but they are back and those of you who have given cupboard space to that large copper jelly mold for so long now will finally be vindicated.

I bet a surprising number of us have aunty's Victorian mousse or blancmange mold squirreled away in the attic, the tiered curvilinear form of la belle époque that we couldn't bear to part with, so dust it off as it's about to come into its own. You can embellish this blancmange with sugared almonds—pink, white, and silver all look great. Then think of the vibrant pastel shades of Ladurée's macaroons, deep yellow-hued lemon and the dark pink of mixed red fruits.

# raspberry blancmange

Peanut oil or vegetable
  oil for brushing
3 gelatin leaves, cut into broad strips
  (or 1 envelope granulated gelatin,
  see page 47)
14 ounces raspberries
  (about 2½–3 cups)
1 cup confectioners' sugar, sifted
1¼ cups heavy cream

## For serving
Macaroons
Sugared almonds

## Serves 6

Lightly brush a 2½-cup gelatin mold with oil. Place the gelatin strips in a bowl, cover with cold water, and let soak for 5 minutes, then drain.

Whizz the raspberries and sugar together in a blender, then press the puree through a strainer to remove the seeds. Gently heat the cream in a small pan until it feels hot to the touch. Add the gelatin and stir until it dissolves, then stir in the raspberry puree. Pour the cream into the mold, cover, and chill overnight.

To turn out the blancmange, briefly dip the mold into a sink of hot water and run a knife around the inside edges at the top. Place a plate or board over the mold and invert it, gently easing the blancmange out. This can be done in advance, in which case cover and chill it until required.

Shortly before serving, decorate with macaroons and sugared almonds.

There's a small group of fruits that you only have to conjure in your mind for your mouth to start watering. Rhubarb, gooseberries, red currants, and lemons come alive as soon as you challenge their sourness with an equally large dose of sugar, and even better the same amount of cream. My heart sinks when I come across gooseberry and rhubarb sauces to serve with salmon and other savory dishes; I can see the rationale but it never quite works in the way that a creamy fool does, which is home for both fruits. You can make the fool up to 24 hours in advance. The cookies are a little added extra, yummy with any creamy little pudding.

# rhubarb fool

### Fool
18 ounces rhubarb, trimmed
    and cut into ¾-inch lengths
    (about 5–6 cups)
⅔ cup sugar
2 cups whipping cream
2 tablespoons Cointreau

### Serves 6

### Poppyseed cookies
½ cup all-purpose flour
2 tablespoons sugar
¼ cup (½ stick) unsalted butter, diced
Pinch of sea salt or kosher salt
½ tablespoon poppyseeds
1 medium egg yolk
Vegetable oil, for greasing

### Makes 15–20

Place the rhubarb in a medium pan with the sugar, cover, and gently heat for 10 minutes, stirring it halfway through, until it has softened and given out its juices. Simmer uncovered for another 20–30 minutes until you have a thick, dry puree, stirring occasionally especially towards the end to make sure it doesn't stick. Transfer the rhubarb to a large bowl and let cool.

Whisk the cream with the Cointreau in a large bowl until stiff; I use an electric hand-held beater. Fold it into the rhubarb puree in three goes to give a marbled effect and transfer to a large serving bowl, glasses, or individual dishes, and cover and chill until required.

To make the cookies, put the flour, sugar, butter, salt, and poppyseeds in the bowl of a food processor and reduce to crumbs. Add the egg yolk and whizz the food processor to bring the dough together into a ball. Wrap in plastic wrap and chill for 1 hour.

Preheat the oven to 400°F and oil a cookie sheet. Knead the dough until pliable, then thinly roll it out on a lightly floured surface, about ⅛-inch thick. Cut out cookies using a 2-inch round cookie cutter, rolling the dough twice, and lay these ½ inch apart on the cookie sheet. Bake for 9–12 minutes until a pale gold, then remove and let the cookies cool on the tray. Transfer them to a plate using a spatula. They will keep well in a covered container for several days.

Travel back to the court at Versailles and the way powdered and jeweled young ladies broke into those tiered blancmanges using their fingers, at least on celluloid, which I've always fancied doing if I ever had the occasion to. For the full fantasy, buy up the sugared roses, the ribbon, the baby meringues, and put your vintage brocade shoes on.

# rose folly

12 gelatin leaves, cut into broad
   strips (or 4 envelopes granulated
   gelatin, see page 47)
2½ cups milk
3 tablespoons rosewater
1 cup sugar (refined)
Zest of 1 lemon, removed with a
   potato peeler
2½ cups whipping cream
Pink or peach food coloring liquid
   or paste

## For serving
Baby meringues
Candied rose petals or sugar roses

## Serves 8

Place the gelatin strips in a bowl, cover with cold water, and soak for 5 minutes, then drain. Bring the milk, rosewater, sugar, and lemon zest to a boil, stirring until the sugar dissolves. Remove from the heat, add the gelatin, and stir until it dissolves, then let it cool for about 1 hour to room temperature.

Strain the cooled milk. Whip the cream in a large bowl until stiff; I use a hand-held electric beater, then gradually beat in the milk, and color the mixture a pastel shade of pink or peach with a very little food coloring.

Lightly brush an 8-inch soufflé dish with oil, and four ⅔-cup ramekins. Fill the ramekins with the cream mixture, and pour the rest into the soufflé dish. Cover and chill overnight.

To assemble the blancmange, briefly dip the soufflé dish into a sink of hot water, run a knife around the edge, place a plate or board over the mold and invert it. Next run a knife around the edge of each ramekin, and ease the blancmange out, arranging 3 of them in a triangle on top of the large blancmange. Place the fourth on top in the center, so that you have three tiered layers. This can be done an hour or two in advance, in which case cover and chill the assembly.

Just before serving, decorate with baby meringues, and candied rose petals or sugar roses.

A silky rose-scented mousse scattered with pistachios and every bit as luxurious as a fine ice cream. I suppose anything that's pale pink and perfumed comes with its fair share of girl appeal, though you can always forego the color.

# chilled rose soufflés

2 gelatin leaves, cut into broad strips
   (or ¾ envelope granulated gelatin,
   see page 47)
¾ cup milk
5 medium egg yolks
⅔ cup sugar

1 tablespoon rosewater
Pink or red food coloring liquid or
   paste (optional)
1¼ cups whipping cream
2 tablespoons finely chopped pistachios

### Serves 6

Place the gelatin strips in a bowl, cover with cold water, and let soak for 5 minutes, then drain.

Bring the milk to a boil in a small nonstick pan. Whisk the egg yolks and sugar together in a bowl, then whisk in the milk. Return the mixture to the pan and cook over a low heat, stirring almost constantly until the mixture thickens into a thin custard that coats the back of a spoon. Strain through a fine mesh strainer onto the gelatin and stir to dissolve, then stir in the rosewater. If you like, you can also color it pink with a little food coloring. Cover the surface with plastic wrap and let it cool completely, about 1 hour.

Use an electric beater to stiffly whip the cream in a large bowl, then fold in the cooled custard in two goes. Divide the mousse between six ⅔-cup ramekins or other little bowls or cups. Place the dishes in a roasting dish or on a small tray, cover with plastic wrap and chill overnight until set. Shortly before serving, scatter some pistachios in the center.

This is the stuff of relaxed kitchen suppers with just a handful of friends or family who won't mind if you retreat into a deep concentration at the stove and keep them waiting for ten minutes before it's ready. It's always worth waiting for.

# zabaglione

4 medium organic egg yolks
¼ cup sugar
scant ½ cup Marsala wine

## Serves 6

Whisk together the egg yolks and sugar in a largish bowl that will allow for the zabaglione to swell into a foamy mass. Set the bowl over a pan with a little simmering water in it, add the Marsala and, using a hand-held electric beater (you can do this with an ordinary whisk but it will take much longer), start beating the mixture on a medium speed. It will rise and become frothy relatively quickly, but continue to whisk the mixture until it is the consistency of whipped cream. This will take about 5–8 minutes. Remove the bowl from the heat and serve.

Unlike a soufflé, zabaglione doesn't sink instantly when removed from the heat, and will stand around for a few minutes.

A mixing of cultures here, panna cotta can only benefit from the added flavor of a little Gallic crème fraîche over normal cream. These desserts are rich by design, and wallow in a shot of eau de vie, tempered by the sharp burst of red currants.

# panna cotta
# with red currants

2 gelatin leaves, cut into broad strips
   (or ⅔ envelope of granulated gelatin,
   see page 47)
2 cups crème fraîche (if unavailable,
   use heavy cream)
⅓ cup sugar
1 vanilla bean, slit
4 tablespoons kirsch or other fruit
   eau de vie
8 sprigs of red currants

Serves 4

Place the gelatin strips in a bowl, cover with cold water, and soak for 5 minutes, then drain. Pour a few tablespoons of boiling water over the gelatin and stir until it dissolves.

Place the crème fraîche and sugar in a small pan and gently heat until the cream melts and the sugar dissolves, then remove from the heat. Open out the vanilla bean and scrape out the seeds with a small sharp knife. Blend a little of the crème fraîche with the seeds and blend this back into the rest of the cream in the saucepan.

Stir a little of the cream into the gelatin, and then return this to the rest of the cream. Pour the mixture into four small glasses or ⅔-cup ramekin dishes. Cover and chill in the fridge for several hours or overnight until set.

To serve, run a knife around the edge of each cream to loosen it, and then turn it out onto a plate. Pour a tablespoon of eau de vie over each cream. String the red currant sprigs (see page 171), and scatter the berries around the sides of each panna cotta, or drape two red currant sprigs on top of each serving.

The thin layer of caramel on top of a crème brûlée that invites us to dip in our spoons is all but impossible to achieve without a small blowtorch, which is one piece of kitchen equipment most of us can live without, given its infrequent use. I prefer to make the caramel in a saucepan and drizzle just a little over them, it looks even prettier and you still get that burnt sugar crunch.

# crème brûlée

## Cream

6 medium egg yolks
3 heaped tablespoons superfine sugar
1 vanilla bean, chopped
2½ cups heavy cream

Confectioners' sugar, for dusting

## Caramel

⅔ cup sugar

## Serves 6

Preheat the oven to 325°F. Whizz all the ingredients for the cream together in a blender, and strain through a strainer into a bowl or large measuring cup. Divide between six ⅔-cup ramekins and place them in a roasting pan. Pour hot but not boiling water into the roasting pan until it's two thirds of the way up the sides of the custard cups. Bake for 1–1¼ hours until lightly golden on the surface. They should be set and may gently wobble if moved from side to side, but should not appear to still be liquid. Remove the ramekins from the roasting pan and let them cool to room temperature.

Gently heat the sugar for the caramel in a small saucepan (do <u>not</u> use a nonstick one as the crystals can scratch it), until about half of it has liquified and started to color, then gently stir it. Watch carefully, stirring frequently until it is a deep gold, then remove from the heat. Liberally dust the creams with confectioners' sugar through a small sifter, then drizzle a spoonful of caramel over each one. It should set hard within minutes. Cover and chill for a couple of hours.

## blueberry compote

An alternative to the caramel top is to serve crème brûlée with a fruit compote, blueberries for instance. Place 2 cups blueberries and ¼ cup sugar in a small pan over a low heat, and gently cook for 5–8 minutes, stirring occasionally, until the sugar has melted and formed a syrup with the juice from the blueberries. Transfer the fruit and syrup to a bowl, add a squeeze of lemon juice, and let cool. Spoon the blueberries and syrup over the crème brûlées–you can do this before or after chilling.

A light healthy girl's dessert, one that's also yummy mid-morning with an espresso. For the full crunch, it needs to be eaten soon after it's assembled, but you can always make up the yogurt in advance. It's still very good once the oats soften though, in which case, just cover and chill it.

# layered passionfruit and yogurt crunch

2 cups Greek yogurt (or other whole-milk yogurt)
⅓ cup confectioners' sugar, sifted
1 tablespoon lemon juice
2 passionfruit, cut in half
½ cup granola

Serves 4

Blend the yogurt with the confectioners' sugar and lemon juice. Spoon half of this into the bottom of four 6-ounce glasses, spoon half the passionfruit seeds over it, then scatter the granola on top. Spoon the remaining yogurt over that and drizzle the rest of the passionfruit seeds over the top.

Don't take the name too literally, but this does stand the test of a few days in the fridge, firming up as time goes on. Its charm hasn't dimmed since its heyday—it's certainly been around since my childhood—and it's hard to see it ever going away.

What has disappeared in England, however, are those blocks of chocolate chip mint ice cream, a resoundingly fond memory, that I sometimes summon up by stirring tiny splinters of dark chocolate into the syllabub, which has the same appeal.

Using a large sharp knife, finely slice 1½ ounces dark chocolate to give you about ¼ cup chocolate splinters. Set aside a scant tablespoon, and fold the rest into the syllabub, then scatter a little of the reserved chocolate into the center of each one before chilling.

# everlasting lemon syllabub

Juice of 1 lemon

1 heaped teaspoon finely grated
   lemon zest

2 tablespoons brandy

¼ cup superfine sugar

¾ cup heavy cream

⅓ cup sweet white wine

Jellied lemon slices for decoration

Cigarettes russes or other delicate
   cookies, for serving (optional)

## Serves 4

Place the lemon juice, the zest, brandy, and the sugar in a bowl and leave it for at least 2 hours. Stir the mixture to dissolve the sugar, but don't worry if it doesn't dissolve completely.

Whip the cream in a bowl until it just starts to hold its shape; I use a hand-held electric beater, and add the wine in about three goes, beating between each addition. If the wine is added too quickly the mixture can split, so it's important to do it gradually. Finally add the lemon and sugar mixture and beat to a thick, fluffy syllabub.

Spoon into glasses, decorate with a couple of lemon slices, cover, and chill for several hours. The syllabub will keep well in the fridge for several days. Serve with cigarettes russes, or some other lacy cookie, if you wish.

In my mind, this has a slight edge over a crème brûlée (see page 86)—it's not as rich, but the liquid caramel is a sure fire thing, the easiest part of it. Don't stint on the vanilla here, the sacrifice of a whole bean is eminently worth it, a light wobbly custard laced with tiny seeds.

# crème caramel

## Custard

3 cups milk

1 vanilla bean, slit

5 large eggs

⅓ cup sugar

## Caramel

⅔ cup sugar (refined)

2 tablespoons water

Serves 6

Pour the milk into a small pan. Open up the vanilla bean and scrape out the seeds with a small sharp knife; add these to the milk, along with the bean. Bring to a boil, then remove from the heat and let it infuse while you make the caramel.

Place the sugar for the caramel in another small pan—<u>not</u> a nonstick pan—with the water. Bring to a boil, and stir now and again until the sugar has dissolved, then simmer until it turns a deep toffee-apple gold, stirring as it begins to color at the edges. Pour it over the bottom of six small bowls or ⅔-cup ramekins and let it harden for about 15 minutes.

Preheat the oven to 300°F. Bring the milk back to a boil. Whisk the eggs and sugar for the custard in a large bowl, then whisk in the hot milk, and strain it all through a strainer into a large measuring cup or pitcher. Place the ramekins in a roasting pan. Pour the custard into the ramekins, covering the caramel bottoms. Pour cold water into the roasting pan until it comes two thirds of the way up the sides of the ramekins, and bake for 1 hour. Remove the ramekins from the roasting pan, run a small sharp knife around the inside edges of each ramekin, and carefully peel off the skin that has formed. Loosely cover with plastic wrap and let cool, then cover and chill for several hours. They keep well for a couple of days.

To serve, run a knife around the edge of each crème caramel, place a plate on top, and invert.

trifles

Good old English trifles are a deep-sea dive, down through a glassy surface of cream and custard to an underworld of hidden treasures that ends in a booze-soaked syrupy bed of sponge cake. Over the centuries they have been shaped by fashion, and bizarrely, have come full circle. If the intervening years at the turn of the 20th century saw "de trop" trifles that called for three different types of jam, as well as marmalade and several types of wine and liqueur, today the finest reflect the 18th-century tradition of Hannah Glasse's day of custard topped with a layer of syllabub.

I have always loved making—or rather creating—trifles. Their forte lies with the artistic license of dreaming up the different layers. The bottom layer can be anything that's willing to soak up the liquor. The "trifle sponges" sold in England are obviously designed for the task, sweet and so dry you would never dream of eating them on their own. And ladyfingers are another material, or it could be a light sponge cake for something truly soft. I particularly like the contemporary touch of using jelly roll slices, propped upright like wheels around the inside of the bowl, that wittily takes care of two ingredients in one.

Then there's the booze, the jam, the fruit, the amaretti for that vintage savor once provided by ratafia cookies, and the deep deep bank of whatever syllabub, custard, or whipped cream you have chosen. An all-singing, all-dancing trifle will have at least two if not three of these creamy layers, but that's going to take you several hours to assemble. And if it has to be just one, then my vote goes to syllabub, featherlight and laced with sweet wine and liqueurs, with the advantage of slowly giving these sublime liquids up to the sponge cake layer in the day or two after it's made. So while the cake softens, the syllabub firms to a mousse, making it a triumph to eat after its spell of slumbering in the fridge.

There is something of the age of innocence about this trifle. Its simplicity takes me back to the trifles my mother used to make. If there is any difference it is the syllabub in lieu of custard—light and fluffy, and heady with sweet sherry and liqueur.

# old-fashioned sherry trifle

### Trifle

4 oranges (medium rather
  than navel)
2½ tablespoons sugar
6 trifle sponges (or ladyfingers or
  sponge cake)
scant ½ cup seedless raspberry jam

### Syllabub

Finely grated zest of 1 orange,
  plus 2 tablespoons juice
Good squeeze of lemon juice
½ cup sweet sherry
2 tablespoons Cointreau
⅓ cup confectioners' sugar, sifted
1¼ cups heavy cream

### For decoration

Soft amaretti
Confectioners' sugar, for dusting
Gold or silver dragees (optional)

### Serves 8

To make the trifle, cut 2 of the oranges in half and squeeze their juice into a small pan. Add the sugar and heat over medium until reduced to about 3 tablespoons. Arrange the trifle sponges on the bottom of an 8-inch glass bowl that's at least 3¼ inches deep, cutting to fit and squeezing them in. Splash the orange syrup over them. Place the jam in another bowl and work it with a spoon until smooth, then spread it over the sponges.

Slice off the skin and outer pith from the remaining 2 oranges. Run a small sharp knife between the segments to remove them from the membranes, and place the skinned segments in a strainer over a bowl. Scatter the segments and their juice over the trifle sponges.

To make the syllabub, whisk the orange zest and juice with the lemon juice, sherry, Cointreau, and confectioners' sugar in a large bowl. Slowly beat in the cream and continue to beat until you have a light and fluffy syllabub. While it needs to be the consistency of softly whipped cream, take care not to over-beat otherwise it can separate; I use a hand-held electric beater. Smooth the syllabub over the trifle sponge. Cover with plastic wrap and chill overnight. During this time the syllabub will firm up, and the juices will soak into the sponge. Just before serving, decorate with amaretti, a dusting of confectioners' sugar, and dragees, if you wish.

Jelly rolls could have been custom-made to line the bottom of a trifle, a ready-made all-in-one of sponge cake and jam that couldn't look prettier standing up like wheels around the inside of a glass bowl. I prefer to leave the pits in the cherries in this recipe to preserve the maiden whiteness of the cream, and the plump fruit gives the trifle a wholesome rusticity.

# strawberry and cherry trifle with almonds

### Trifle

14 ounces jelly roll

2 tablespoons amaretto

½ cup strawberry jam

2¾ cups strawberries, hulled

### Syllabub

Finely grated zest of 1 orange,
   plus 2 tablespoons juice

Good squeeze of lemon juice

½ cup sweet wine

2 tablespoons brandy

⅓ cup confectioners' sugar,
   sifted

1¼ cups heavy cream

### For decoration

1¼ cups cherries

⅓ cup toasted almonds*

confectioners' sugar

### Serves 6

Line the sides of an 8-inch-wide glass bowl, at least 3¼ inches deep, with ¾-inch-thick slices of jelly roll, placed upright. Cut the rest of the cake 1½ inches thick and line the bottom. Splash the amaretto over it. Strain the jam through a strainer into a bowl, slice the strawberries, then fold them into the jam. Spoon this over the cake in the middle.

To make the syllabub, whisk the orange zest and juice with the lemon juice, sweet wine, brandy, and confectioners' sugar in a large bowl. Slowly beat in the cream in a thin stream, and continue to beat until you have a light and fluffy syllabub. While it needs to be the consistency of softly whipped cream, take care not to over-beat otherwise it can separate; I use a hand-held electric beater. Smooth the syllabub over the jam-covered cake. Cover with plastic wrap and chill overnight. During this time the syllabub will firm up, and the juices will soak into the cake.

Just before serving, decorate with the cherries and almonds and a dusting of confectioners' sugar.

*To toast almonds, scatter them evenly into a small baking pan and toast for 8–10 minutes in an oven preheated to 400°F.

## traditional trifle

Replace the jelly roll with 6 trifle sponges, cutting to fit, and squeezing them in.

Deliciously silky and cooling, one for those who reckon the best bits of a trifle are the boozy cake and custard and can skip the jam and fruit. Though you could also scatter a handful of raspberries or blackberries over each bowl. Do buy your cake if you don't have anything homemade at hand, though try to avoid those mass-produced sponge cakes: you want something with a little integrity.

# italian trifle

6 large egg yolks

1 cup confectioners' sugar, sifted

½ cup all-purpose flour, sifted

2¾ cups whole milk

3 strips of lemon peel

1½ teaspoons vanilla extract

4 tablespoons dark rum

8 ounces plain sponge cake or
   pound cake, cut into ½-inch slices

Cocoa powder, for dusting

## Serves 6

Whisk the egg yolks and confectioners' sugar together in a medium nonstick pan until smooth, and then whisk in the flour, a third at a time, until you have a thick creamy paste.

Bring the milk to a boil in a small pan with the lemon peel, and whisk it into the egg mixture, a little at a time initially, until it is all incorporated. Return the pan to a low heat and cook for a few minutes until the custard thickens, stirring vigorously with a wooden spoon to disperse any lumps that form, if necessary you can give it a quick whisk. The custard shouldn't actually boil, but the odd bubble will ensure it's hot enough to thicken properly. Cook it for a few minutes longer after it thickens, again stirring constantly. Remove the custard from the heat and stir in the vanilla and half the rum. Discard the lemon zest, pour the custard into a bowl, cover the surface with plastic wrap, and let cool.

To assemble the trifle, give the custard a stir with a spoon to smooth it, then spread a couple of tablespoons in the bottom of an 8-inch glass bowl, at least 3¼ inches deep (it can also be assembled in individual glass dishes). Break up some of the sliced cake and arrange evenly in the bottom of the bowl to partially cover it. Sprinkle a little of the remaining rum over it, then smooth a third of the custard over that. Repeat until you have three layers of cake and three of custard, ending with custard. Cover the trifle with plastic wrap and chill for at least 2 hours. It can also be made the night before.

To serve, liberally dust the surface with cocoa using a sifter.

Every now and again I chance upon quinces outside the Middle Eastern stores close to where I live, but for the most part rely on membrillo or quince paste when I need something of this perfumed fruit. You can use brandy if you don't have Poire William.

# pear and quince trifle

1¼ cups water

¾ cup sugar

1 vanilla bean, slit, or 1 teaspoon
   vanilla extract

2 Comice pears

2 tablespoons Poire William

2½ ounces ladyfingers

⅓ cup membrillo

1 tablespoon lemon juice

## Syllabub

Finely grated zest of 1 orange,
   plus 2 tablespoons juice

Good squeeze of lemon juice

½ cup sweet wine

2 tablespoons Cointreau

⅓ cup confectioners' sugar

1¼ cups heavy cream

## For decoration

3 tablespoons toasted slivered
   almonds (see page 97)

Serves 6–8

Place the water, the sugar, and vanilla in a small pan and bring to a boil. Peel and cut the pears in half, and add them to the syrup so that as far as possible they are submerged. Cover with a circle of baking parchment and poach until the pears are tender when pierced with a skewer, this can take 4–15 minutes depending upon their ripeness. Let them cool in the syrup, then remove and drain thoroughly, quarter, core, and finely slice them lengthwise. Mix 2 tablespoons of the syrup with the Poire William eau de vie.

Arrange the ladyfingers, sugared-side up, in the bottom of an 8-inch glass bowl, at least 3¼ inches deep. Drizzle the brandied syrup over them, and scatter the pears on top. Gently heat the membrillo with the lemon juice in a small pan, working it with a spoon until it's smooth and melted. Smear this over the pears.

To make the syllabub, whisk the orange zest and juice with the squeeze of lemon juice, sweet wine, Cointreau, and confectioners' sugar in a bowl. Slowly beat in the cream, and continue to beat until you have a light and fluffy syllabub. While it needs to be the consistency of whipped cream, take care not to over-beat otherwise it can separate; I use a hand-held electric beater. Pour the syllabub over the trifle and smooth the surface, cover with plastic wrap, and chill for several hours or ideally overnight. (You can, in fact, make it up to two days beforehand.) During this time the syllabub will firm up, and the juices will soak into the ladyfingers.

To serve, scatter the almonds over the top.

A trifle full of wintery sentiments, that looks to Scotland for inspiration from its famed dessert of toasted steel-cut oats, cream, and Scotch.

# cranachan trifle

3 trifle sponges (or sponge cake), sliced
⅓ cup raspberry jam
1½ cups raspberries
5 ounces crumbled oat bars—about 1⅓ cups (see below)

## Syllabub

finely grated zest of 1 orange, plus ½ cup smooth fresh orange juice
3½ tablespoons Scotch
⅓ cup confectioners' sugar, sifted
1¼ cups heavy cream

## Serves 6–8

Arrange the sliced sponges in the bottom of an 8-inch glass bowl, at least 3¼ inches deep. Work the jam with a spoon until smooth, then stir in the raspberries, reserving a few for decoration. Spoon the fruit mixture over the sponge, then scatter the crumbled oat bars on top.

To make the syllabub, whisk the orange zest and juice with the Scotch and confectioners' sugar in a large bowl. Slowly beat in the cream in a thin stream, and continue to beat until you have a light and fluffy syllabub. While it needs to be the consistency of softly whipped cream, take care not to over-beat otherwise it can separate; I use a hand-held electric beater. Smooth the syllabub over the trifle. Cover with plastic wrap and chill overnight. During this time the syllabub will firm up, and the juices will soak into the sponge.

Just before serving, decorate with a few raspberries, and a dusting of confectioners' sugar, if you wish.

## oat bars

For divinely chewy flapjacks, preheat the oven to 350°F. Gently melt 1 cup plus 1 tablespoon diced salted butter with a scant cup demerara sugar and 6 tablespoons golden syrup (use corn syrup if golden is unavailable) in a medium pan over a medium heat. Stir in 3½ cups old-fashioned oats (I prefer processed ones here to anything too butch and nutty). Tip the mixture into a 9-inch square pan or equivalent size, pressing it down, and bake for 20 minutes. Let cool and then cut into squares.

This is summer pudding in trifle form, which I think I could come to love even more than the classic British summer pudding. Ladyfingers are layered with the compote and soak up all the juices, and the whole thing is smothered in cream—so easy.

# summer pudding trifle

18 ounces red currants
(about 4½–5 cups)
¾ cup sugar
1½ pounds raspberries (about
4½ cups), plus a few extra for
decoration
5 ounces ladyfingers
(about 1½ cups)
1¼ cups heavy cream,
whipped to soft peaks
Confectioners' sugar, for dusting
(optional)

## Serves 6

String the currants (see page 171) into a small pan using a fork, add the sugar, and gently heat together, stirring occasionally, for 4–6 minutes until the fruit is soft but still retains its shape, and is sitting in a pool of syrup. Place half the currants in a strainer and press the juice into a bowl and then return it to the pan, discarding the crushed berries. Fold in the raspberries, stir well, and heat very gently for a minute or two, not to cook them but to encourage them to release their juices, gently turning them once. Transfer the compote to a bowl and let it cool.

Arrange half the ladyfingers in the bottom of an 8-inch glass bowl at least 3¼ inches deep. Spoon half of the compote over the ladyfingers, then repeat with the remaining ladyfingers and compote. Cover and chill for a couple of hours, then smooth the whipped cream over the surface, cover, and chill for another couple of hours or overnight.

Just before serving, decorate with a few raspberries, and if you like, give them a flurry of confectioners' sugar.

# all-white trifle

## Sponge cake
4 medium organic egg whites
Pinch of sea salt or kosher salt
½ teaspoon cream of tartar
1 cup confectioners' sugar, sifted
½ cup all-purpose flour, sifted

## Trifle
1 x 14-ounce can pears in syrup
3 tablespoons Poire William
  or brandy
6 meringue nests (3 ounces),
  crumbled

## Mousse
2 cups mascarpone
4 medium organic egg whites
¼ cup superfine sugar
1 vanilla bean, slit,
  or 1 teaspoon vanilla extract

## For decoration
6 amaretti
1 tablespoon toasted almonds
Confectioners' sugar, for dusting

## Sauce
¾ cup black currant jam
1 tablespoon lemon juice

## Serves 6–8

Preheat the oven to 325°F. Beat the egg whites in a large bowl with the salt and cream of tartar until risen; I use a hand-held electric beater. Sprinkle in the sugar a couple of tablespoons at a time, beating for about 20 seconds with each addition. Fold the sifted flour into the batter in two goes, then transfer the batter to a buttered 8-inch cake pan at least 2 inches deep, with a removable bottom. Bake the cake for 30–35 minutes until lightly golden on the surface, springy to the touch, and shrinking from the sides. Run a knife around the edge of the cake and let it cool in the pan. Slice off its top with a bread knife, then cut it off the bottom of the pan and trim the sides of any golden edges so you are left with all white cake. Slice this horizontally into two thin layers with the bread knife.

Crumble the meringue nests into a bowl. Mix 5 tablespoons of the pear syrup with the Poire William eau de vie or brandy, and sprinkle half of it over the crumbled meringues. Thinly slice the pears. To prepare the mousse, beat the mascarpone in a bowl until smooth and creamy. If it seems hard, whizz it in the bowl of a food processor. In another bowl, beat the egg whites until they hold their shape, then gradually sprinkle in the sugar and beat well with each addition until you have a glossy meringue. Fold this in three goes into the mascarpone until you have a fluffy mousse. Open up the vanilla bean, scrape out the seeds with a small sharp knife, and work them into the mousse, or stir in the extract.

To assemble, smear a spoon of the mousse over the bottom of an 8-inch glass bowl, at least 3¼ inches deep. Lay one cake layer on top and sprinkle half the remaining brandied syrup over it. Scatter half the crumbled meringues on top, then half the pears, and smooth over that just under half of the mousse to allow plenty of the mousse for the top. Repeat with the remaining ingredients. Cover and chill for at least 2 hours (or it can be made a day or two in advance).

Shortly before serving, pile the amaretti in the center, scatter the almonds over it, then dust with confectioners' sugar. To make the sauce, spoon the jam into a bowl and give it a stir, then blend in the lemon juice. Serve with the trifle.

In this variation on a traditional theme, a mascarpone mousse stands in for custard or syllabub, bringing it right up to the present day on our chronological calendar of the evolution of these lovely desserts, by borrowing from the Italian pantry.

# modern sherry trifle

6 trifle sponges (or use ladyfingers)
½ cup sweet sherry
¾ cup black currant jam
1 tablespoon lemon juice
2 large oranges

## Mousse

3 medium organic eggs, separated
¼ cup superfine sugar
1¾ cups mascarpone
½ teaspoon vanilla extract
  (optional)

## For decoration

Silver dragees, or toasted
  slivered almonds (see page 97),
  optional
Confectioners' sugar (optional)
Silver balls (optional)

## Serves 6–8

Arrange the trifle sponges over the bottom of an 8-inch glass bowl, at least 3¼ inches deep, and sprinkle with the sherry. Combine the jam and lemon juice in a bowl and smooth it over the sponges. Cut the skin and outer pith off the oranges and run a sharp knife between the segments to remove them from the membranes. Scatter the skinned segments over the jam.

To make the mousse, whisk the egg yolks and sugar in a bowl, then beat in the mascarpone, and vanilla extract if using. Using clean beaters, beat the egg whites until stiff; I use a hand-held electric beater, and fold into the mascarpone mixture. Smooth this over the top of the trifle, cover, and chill for several hours. It will keep well for a couple of days.

Shortly before serving, either scatter with silver dragees or toasted almonds (dusting them with confectioners' sugar) or with a few silver balls.

# chocolate desserts

Chocolate is the lowest common denominator that spans every age group, culture, and occasion. It even draws in the "no thank yous" who don't normally eat dessert. Starting with the smallest and traveling up, chocolate mousse, which consists simply of eggs and chocolate, is a dessert no one should feel any more ashamed of dishing up than strawberries and cream. A touch more sophisticated are the petit pots au chocolat—by definition edible silk that melts in the mouth. Either of these delectable little numbers can be spiced up with vanilla, cinnamon, eaux de vie, and sticky liqueurs.

Before we get to hearty baked desserts, there is a halfway house: chocolate pudding cakes are as delicious as they are clever. With a thin crust of fluffy cake encasing a thick chocolate sauce, they remind me of Lemon Surprise Pudding cake, which I have always suspected rose from the ashes of a failed soufflé. I can't help but feel that when someone first came up with "Chocolate Pudding Cakes" they had simply underestimated the cooking time of a baked cake—in which case, long may people continue to make mistakes in the kitchen.

A little more on the gutsy side is a tray-baked chocolate cake that can be cut into hulking squares and served with lashings of salty caramel sauce. Finally, when you fancy a small chocolatey farewell to dinner with a cup of coffee, then a tiny sliver of chocolate torte—that nemesis moment—or a gooey brownie is the answer. You can always wrap up the leftover to send home for any offspring not included, which might even encourage them to allow your guests out again.

Petit pots have always had the sophisticated edge over chocolate mousse with their exquisitely silky texture, achieved here by combining dark chocolate with a little milk. These particular little pots have Spanish overtones with their hint of spice and a chocolate almond on top. But for diehard chocoholics, you could serve them austerely, minus the spice and decoration, and for that matter, minus the crème fraîche, too.

# petit pots au chocolat

1 cup heavy cream

¾ cup whole milk

4 medium organic egg yolks, whisked in a bowl

3 ounces milk chocolate, broken into pieces (about ½ cup)

5½ ounces dark chocolate (about 50% cocoa), broken into pieces (about ¾–1 cup)

½ teaspoon vanilla extract

⅓ teaspoon ground cinnamon

½ cup crème fraîche (if unavailable, use heavy cream)

6 chocolate almonds (optional)

Serves 6

Bring the cream and milk to a boil in a small nonstick pan, and whisk it into the egg yolks which should thicken into a thin custard instantly. Strain this through a strainer into another bowl, cover the surface with plastic wrap and let cool.

Gently melt the chocolate in the top of a double boiler over a little simmering water. Whisk in the cooled custard in two goes, then stir in the vanilla and cinnamon. Divide this between six ⅔-cup ramekins or other little dishes or coffee cups of a similar size. Cover and chill for several hours. Drop a heaped teaspoon of crème fraîche on the top of each little cup and decorate with a chocolate almond, if you wish. Cover and chill for another few hours or overnight.

However simple, you can't go wrong with chocolate mousse for dessert, whatever the occasion. Everybody loves it. It has an elementary appeal, there's no point in complicating it: chocolate, eggs, and a little liquid something. The coffee suggested could just as well be brandy, Cointreau, or Tia Maria. Of course it doesn't have to be dressed up, but here are some suggestions for serving it up at a party.

# chocolate mousse

9 ounces dark chocolate (about 50% cocoa), broken into pieces (about 1½ cups)

6 medium organic eggs, separated

2 tablespoons strong black coffee

Chocolate coffee beans, thins, or buttons, for decoration (optional)

Cocoa, for dusting

Cigarettes russes or other dessert cookies, for serving (optional)

**Serves 6**

Gently melt the chocolate in the top of a double boiler over a little simmering water. The melted chocolate should be at room temperature, so if necessary, let it cool for a few minutes before stirring in the egg yolks and then the coffee.

In another large bowl, beat the egg whites until they are stiff; I use a hand-held electric beater. Mix a couple of tablespoons into the chocolate mixture to loosen it, then fold in the rest in two goes, as lightly as possible.

Transfer the mousse to a serving bowl or individual bowls or glasses, smoothing the surface. Decorate with chocolate coffee beans, thins, or buttons, or simply dust with cocoa. Cover with plastic wrap and chill for several hours or overnight until firm.

Serve with cigarettes russes or other little dessert cookies, if you like.

I first ate these at La Bastide de Moustiers, Alain Ducasse's enchanting small hotel in the hills of Provence. My husband and I were enjoying a lazy lunch one blue-skied September day, with raw cut-up dipping vegetables, right from the hotel garden, with dips made from crushed local goat cheeses and olives, and a pan of crayfish from the nearby mountain ravine, so fresh they could have swum over, when a whirlwind whipped up from nowhere and a helicopter landed within a few feet of our table, having transported some incoming diners from the baking plains below. So these little custards that we ate for dessert have always held "another world" glamour for me. I seem to recall there was a little coffee custard in the equation too, and some shortbread cookies scented with lavender. But we'll settle for the chocolate and vanilla versions served with Cadbury's chocolate fingers or mini florentines.

# black and white custards

2 cups whole milk

2 cups heavy cream

10 medium organic egg yolks

1 cup sugar

1 vanilla bean, cut up

3 ounces dark chocolate (about 50% cocoa), chopped into small pieces (about ½ cup)

6 tablespoons each dark and white chocolate shavings

Confectioners' sugar and cocoa powder, for dusting

Chocolate fingers or mini florentines, for serving (optional)

## Serves 6

Preheat the oven to 325°F. Bring the milk and the cream to a boil in a small nonstick pan. Whisk the egg yolks and the sugar together in a large bowl, and whisk in the boiled milk. Pour half into another bowl.

Add the vanilla bean to one and let it infuse for 10 minutes. Add the chopped-up chocolate to the other, and leave it for a few minutes. Whisk and strain the two different mixtures into heatproof bowls (I used four 1-pint cupped bowls, to give me two of each flavor, enough for six of us). Place them in a roasting pan with hot but not boiling water that comes two thirds of the way up the sides, and bake for 1 hour 15 minutes. They should be set but may gently wobble if moved from side to side, without appearing liquid. Let the custards cool completely, then cover and chill for several hours or overnight.

Shortly before serving, scatter the dark chocolate shavings over the vanilla custard, and dust with confectioners' sugar, and scatter the white chocolate shavings over the dark chocolate custard and dust with cocoa powder. Serve them with chocolate fingers or florentines for a treat.

While so many desserts demand the respect of being left exactly as they are, tiramisu is just the opposite, a great formula with endless possibilities for playing around, like trifles. I realize that I'm risking the wrath of Italian gourmets here, and perhaps I should have called it something else. But tiramisu is basically a trifle. Here you have ladyfingers soaked in boozy coffee, layered with chocolate mousse in lieu of the usual mascarpone one.

# very chocolatey tiramisu

⅔ cup strong black coffee,
  cooled
5 tablespoons Kahlúa or dark
  rum
1 x quantity chocolate mousse
  (see page 114)
About 4 ounces ladyfingers
Cocoa powder, for dusting

## Serves 6

Combine the coffee and liqueur in a shallow bowl. Smear a couple of tablespoons of the chocolate mousse on the bottom of an 8-inch glass bowl, at least 2½ inches deep. Dip the ladyfingers into the coffee-liqueur mixture until the cookies just start to yield between your fingers, but not so that they are totally sodden.

Cover the bottom of the bowl with a single layer of ladyfingers, smooth half of the mousse on top, then repeat with the remaining half of the ingredients. Cover the surface with plastic wrap and chill for several hours or overnight. Dust with cocoa powder shortly before serving.

Halfway between a "mousse" and "petit pots," just in case you felt a need to bridge the gap. At Eastertime you can turn these into little surprise soufflés by dropping a mini cream egg into each ramekin before filling them. As my nine-year old put it "Nice touch, mum."

# chilled chocolate soufflés

Gently melt the dark chocolate in the top of a double boiler over a little simmering water. Let it cool for a few minutes, then beat in the egg yolks and then gradually whisk in the cream, and the sugar. Using clean beaters, beat the egg whites until they are stiff in a large bowl using an electric beater, and fold them into the chocolate mixture in two or three goes.

Carefully pour the chocolate mixture into six ⅔-cup ramekins. You may find it easiest to transfer the mixture to a large measuring cup or pitcher first. Place the ramekins on a baking tray, loosely cover with plastic wrap, and chill for several hours or overnight until set. To serve, dust the edges of the soufflés with grated chocolate.

THE REAL THING If you want to go the whole hog of a soufflé that's risen above the surface of the dish, then cut out six strips of baking parchment or foil about 2 inches long by the width of the roll. Use these to make a collar for each ramekin, by attaching a piece of adhesive tape to one end and sticking it to the top of the ramekin, then tightly winding it around the bowl and taping it in place. Fill the ramekins about ½ inch above the rim to create the effect of a risen soufflé. In this case the mixture will make 4–5 little cups. Carefully peel off the collars before dusting with chocolate shavings.

6 ounces dark chocolate (about 50% cocoa), broken into pieces (about 1 cup)
3 medium organic eggs, separated
1½ cups whipping cream
2 tablespoons confectioners' sugar, sifted
Grated dark chocolate, for serving

Serves 6

If you are someone who judges all chocolate desserts by "nemesis moments" since first trying London's River Café's seminal cake, then try this one for size. It might be second best, but it's not a bad imitation.

# a nemesis moment

## Cake

⅓ cup all-purpose flour

½ teaspoon baking powder

pinch of salt

¼ cup light brown sugar

3 tablespoons peanut oil

1 medium egg, separated

1 tablespoon espresso, or very strong
   black coffee, cooled

1 tablespoon milk

## Filling

10½ ounces dark chocolate (about 50%
   cocoa), broken into pieces (about
   1½–2 cups)

4 medium eggs, separated

2½ tablespoons sugar

1 cup mascarpone

2 tablespoons Kahlúa or very strong
   black coffee

Edible gold or silver decorations, e.g.,
   buttons, dragees, chocolate stars,
   leaf, etc. (optional)

## Serves 6–8

Heat the oven to 375°F and butter an 8-inch cake pan at least 1½ inches deep with a removable bottom. Sift the flour and sugar into a medium bowl. Add the oil, the egg yolk, espresso, and milk, and beat with a wooden spoon until smooth. With clean beaters, beat the egg white until stiff in another bowl (I use a hand-held electric beater for this) and fold into the batter in two goes. Spoon this into the prepared cake pan, covering the bottom evenly, and give the pan a couple of sharp taps on the counter to let any bubbles rise. Bake for 12–15 minutes until lightly golden, firm when pressed, and shrinking from the sides. Let cool.

Place the chocolate in the top of a double boiler set over a little simmering water and gently let it melt. Remove the chocolate pan from the heat and let the chocolate cool to room temperature if necessary. With clean beaters, beat the egg whites until stiff in a largish bowl using a hand-held electric beater, then beat the egg yolks and sugar in another bowl until very pale and mousse-like.

Add the mascarpone to the melted chocolate and blend it, then fold in the egg yolk mixture, and then the egg whites in two goes. Stir in the Kahlúa or coffee. Smooth the chocolate cream over the cake layer, scatter the gold or silver decorations over it, if you wish, cover, and chill for several hours or overnight.

Run a knife around the inside collar and unclip it to remove it, and serve the torte in slices.

Pudding cakes have come to define everything that is decadent and alluring about chocolate, the way they ooze warm molten goo from around the cakey sides is a bit like having everything chocolatey you ever dreamed of poured into one fantasy: part dense fudgey cake and part thick sticky sauce. Conveniently they can also be prepared well in advance of dinner and popped into the oven ten minutes or so before you want them—for which you will love them even more.

# chocolate pudding cakes

10½ ounces dark chocolate (70% cocoa), broken into pieces (about 1½–2 cups)

⅓ cup (¾ stick) unsalted butter, diced

⅓ cup light brown sugar, plus extra for dusting

5 medium organic eggs

⅓ cup all-purpose flour, sifted

1 tablespoon dark rum (optional)

Vanilla ice cream or crème fraîche, for serving

## Serves 6

Preheat the oven to 400°F and butter six ⅔-cup ramekins. Gently melt the chocolate in the top of a double boiler over a pan with a little simmering water in it.

Place the butter, sugar, eggs, and flour in the bowl of a food processor and whizz to a smooth batter, then add the melted chocolate and whizz again. Finally add the rum, if including. Divide the mixture between the dishes, dust with a little more sugar through a sifter, place on a baking sheet, and bake for 9 minutes, until just starting to rise. There should be a thin rim of cooked cake on the outside, and a sticky river of molten goo inside.

Serve right away, with either ice cream or crème fraîche. The cake batter can also be prepared several hours in advance, in which case cover and chill the little dishes, and bake for 11–12 minutes.

Even though salted caramel seems to be flavor of the month, it's been a tradition in Brittany for years. I've long bought salted caramels in Normandy, and my local deli also sells jars of unctuously soft salted caramel for spreading on toast, something like a dulce de leche. So here we have a great big steaming tray of chocolate sponge cake, crusty and sugary around the top, with the hit of a sauce laced with molasses-rich sugar and crystalline sea salt.

# salty caramel chocolate sponge cake

1 cup (2 sticks) unsalted butter, diced

1 cup sugar, plus 2 tablespoons

3 medium eggs

⅔ cup milk

1¼ cups all-purpose flour, sifted

⅛ teaspoon salt

½ cup cocoa powder, sifted

2 teaspoons baking powder, sifted

## Sauce

½ cup dark brown sugar

½ cup (1 stick) salted butter

⅔ cup heavy cream

## Makes a 12 x 9-inch cake
## Serves more than 8

Preheat the oven to 375°F and butter a 12 x 9 x 1½-inch baking pan. Place the butter and the cup of sugar in the bowl of a food processor and beat together until pale and fluffy. Incorporate the eggs one at a time, scraping down the sides of the bowl if necessary, then add the milk. Don't worry if the mixture appears curdled at this point. Gradually add the flour, salt, cocoa powder, and baking powder through the funnel with the motor running.

Transfer the batter to the baking pan, smoothing the surface. Scatter a couple of tablespoons of sugar over the top and bake for 30 minutes until golden and shrinking slightly from the sides, and a skewer comes out clean from the center. Let it cool in the pan for 20–30 minutes out of the oven, while you make the sauce. Heat the sugar, butter, and cream in a small pan, whisking them until smooth.

Serve the cake cut into squares with the warm caramel sauce spooned over them.

I felt I had to include this recipe, partly because I feel these are the best brownies I've ever baked, but also because a small sliver of brownie makes a great end to lunch or dinner when you want a sugary little something without going the whole hog of getting out the dessert plates and forks. Actually, it doesn't even have to be little: pile them high and wide on the biggest plate you can find.

When I say "good," that is within the context of an addiction to Gü® brownies and that dense texture so fudgey it leaves teethmarks. The secret here is to bake them for just 20 minutes, until they appear slightly cracked and risen around the outside but still gooey in the center. Let them cool for a few hours and then chill for another few hours or overnight, et voilà, no one will know the difference between these and Gü® except these have pistachios in them, and even then the nuts are optional.

If, however, you want something soft and crumbly to eat slightly warm with a scoop of vanilla ice cream, then leave them in the oven that little bit longer, say 25–30 minutes in all, before sticking a skewer into the center. This should come out clean with just a few moist crumbs clinging, without actually coating it.

# pistachio brownies

## Brownies

10½ ounces dark chocolate (about 50% cocoa), broken up (about 1½–2 cups)

¾ cup (1½ sticks) unsalted butter, diced

¾ cup light brown sugar

4 medium eggs, and 1 egg yolk

1 cup ground almonds

¼ teaspoon sea salt or kosher salt

scant cup all-purpose flour

1 heaping teaspoon baking powder

3 tablespoons fresh orange juice

heaping ½ cup shelled pistachios

## Cream (optional)

2½ ounces white chocolate, broken up (⅓–½ cup)

½ tablespoon shelled pistachios

5 tablespoons whipping cream

## Makes 16 brownies

Preheat the oven to 375°F. You need a 9-inch square pan, 1½ inches deep, or the equivalent. If it is nonstick, you needn't butter and flour it—otherwise, butter the pan and dust it with flour.

To make the brownies, gently melt the chocolate with the butter in the top of a double boiler over a pan with a little simmering water in it. Remove from the heat, add the sugar, and stir to combine. Add the eggs and yolk to the chocolate mixture, one by one, beating after each addition, until the mixture is very glossy and amalgamated. Gently fold in the ground almonds and salt, then sift the flour and baking powder over this, and fold in without overmixing. Stir in the orange juice and fold in the pistachios.

Pour the mixture into the pan, and bake for 20–30 minutes (see introduction). Run a knife around the inside edge of the pan, let the cake cool in the pan for several hours, then cut it into 16 squares, or half that size for children's portions.

The brownies will be delicious as they are, but if you want to take them one step further, gently melt the white chocolate in the top of a double boiler over a pan with a little simmering water in it, then remove and let cool to room temperature. Finely crush the pistachios, either using a mortar and pestle or in a food processor. Whip the cream until it is stiff, then gently fold in the cooled melted chocolate. Spoon a rounded teaspoon of this on top of each brownie and crown with a little crushed pistachio. The brownies will keep well in an airtight container for several days, though it is best to wait until the time of eating before scattering the nuts on top.

# pies and crumbles

Time to put on Johnny Cash's "Live At San Quentin" and take your place in the rocker. Pies and crumbles are rooted in the homestead, thick quilts, open fires, and cosying down. They're rough around the edges and that's the appeal: we wouldn't have them any other way. That said, I couldn't resist including a recipe for the Dorchester Hotel's apple crumble just to show what happens when they get dressed for a night on the town.

Pies are firmly headed in the earth-mother direction, the frilly flour-coated apron of the kitchen. Deep red plums compete with Granny Smiths to make one of the most sumptuous pies, slightly soggy crust on the bottom and lashings of rich vanilla custard. Not that pies have to mean pie dough, a thick bank of sponge cake sprinkled with crunchy sugar is another walk down Easy Street. Two of my standbys are apple sponge cake baked in a thin buttery syrup that thickens into a caramel sauce as it cooks, and a rhubarb sponge cake, the fruit hidden beneath a crusty cake wafting steam as you cut into it, like a cobbler.

In real terms, a crumble is like cookie dough that hasn't made it into a ball; a deconstructed cookie laced with butter and sugar, with all the ease that suggests. Its loose texture comes with the potential for adding a smattering of character by way of some oats, nuts, or a little spice.

Summer is almost better than winter for this genre of dessert: juicy red berries, peaches, apricots, and plums are all winners. Evenings are almost always chilly unless you're in the tropics, and a pie or crumble can round off a candle-lit dinner on the terrace in a more welcome way than something flimsy. Lastly, cooked fruit is at its most fragrant 20–30 minutes out of the oven, and still in fine form once cooled, so you can cook these in advance and settle back to the rocker with a good book.

A big no-nonsense apple pie, 100 percent nurture, you can almost see the curl of steam rising from its center as a slipper-clad Mama carries it to the table. Ice cream on top, it has to be here.

# big apple pie

### Sweet pie dough

⅔ cup (1¼ sticks) unsalted butter, softened

¾ cup sugar

2 medium eggs

3 cups all-purpose flour, sifted, plus 1 tablespoon

½ cup ground almonds

### Apples

2 pounds cooking apples, peeled, cored, and sliced

⅔ cup light brown sugar

½ teaspoon ground cinnamon

Finely grated zest of 1 lemon, plus juice of ½ lemon

3 tablespoons unsalted butter

Sugar, for dusting

### Serves 4

To make the pie dough, cream the butter and sugar together in a bowl using a wooden spoon until soft and fluffy. A food processor or mixer will make light work of this. Beat in the eggs until well combined, then gradually add the 3 cups of flour and ground almonds and bring the dough together. Wrap it in plastic wrap and chill for at least 2 hours; it will keep for several days.

Preheat the oven to 375°F. Let the dough come to room temperature for a few minutes, and then knead until pliable. Thinly roll out two thirds of the dough on a lightly floured surface. Use this to line the bottom of a shallow 12-inch (2-quart) pie dish or other shallow ovenproof dish, letting the extra hang over the sides, then trim off the excess. Don't worry if the dough tears and you end up partly pressing it into the dish. Sprinkle the tablespoon of flour over the apples in a bowl and toss, then mix in the brown sugar, spice, lemon zest, and juice. Tip the apples into the pie dish, arranging them evenly, and dot with the butter. Roll out the rest of the dough with the trimmings, and lay it over the top. As the pie dough is quite short and delicate, I find it easiest to wrap it around the rolling pin and lift it up. Press the pie dough together at the rim and trim, leaving ½ inch for shrinkage, then crimp the edge using the tips of your finger and thumb, or the tip of a knife. Cut several diagonal slits in the surface and dust with the sugar. Bake the pie for 40 minutes until golden.

This one's a British aristocrat; rhubarb makes for one of the finest crumbles of all—as do gooseberries during their brief season. It emerges from the oven, its sticky sweet and sour pink juices bubbling like a lazy geyser at the sides, with the promise of the meltingly tender fruit peppered with candied ginger concealed beneath.

# rhubarb crumble

1¾ pounds rhubarb (trimmed weight), cut into 1¼-inch lengths

1½ cups all-purpose flour, plus 2 tablespoons

1 cup demerara sugar (raw sugar)

2 balls preserved ginger, coarsely chopped

1 cup ground almonds

¾ cup (1½ sticks) unsalted butter, chilled and diced

Serves 6

Preheat the oven to 400°F.

Toss the rhubarb in a bowl with the 2 tablespoons of flour, half the sugar, and the ginger, and arrange over the bottom of a 12-inch (2-quart) oval gratin or other shallow ovenproof dish.

Combine the flour, remaining sugar, and ground almonds in a bowl and rub in the butter until you have large crumbs. This can also be done in a food processor, but take care to stop the motor before it turns the crumbs into a dough. Scatter this mixture over the fruit, and bake for 30–35 minutes until the top is golden and crisp, and juices are bubbling up at the sides.

Serve about 20–30 minutes out of the oven. It's also delicious cold.

# peach and pistachio crisp

The most relaxed take on this genre, this one's half baked fruit and half crumble—peaches in a rose-scented syrup with just a smattering of cookie nibs scattered over the top.

½ cup sugar

1 tablespoon rosewater

3 peaches

½ cup all-purpose flour

⅓ cup (¾ stick) unsalted
   butter, diced

⅓ cup shelled pistachios
   (unsalted)

Crème fraîche or heavy cream,
   for serving (optional)

**Serves 6**

Preheat the oven to 400°F.

Pour ⅓ cup boiling water over a third of the sugar in a bowl and stir to dissolve, then stir in the rosewater.

Cut the peaches in half and twist to separate them. Remove the pits; if they don't come out easily use a small sharp knife. Arrange the halves, cut-side up, in a shallow baking dish (I use a 12-inch oval gratin dish) and pour the syrup over the peaches and into the bottom of the dish.

Place the remaining sugar, flour, butter, and pistachios in the bowl of a food processor and reduce to a crumble. Keep the motor running until the mixture starts to cling together into lumps. Scatter the crumble over the peaches: don't worry if some falls to the bottom of the dish. Bake for 40 minutes until golden and crisp on top. There should be a delicious syrupy crumble surrounding the peach halves as well. Serve about 15 minutes out of the oven with a spoon of crème fraîche, if you wish, or at room temperature.

I have always harbored a love of oat bars (called "flapjacks" in England), and here gooey chunks are served crumble-style on a succulent base of apricots and blueberries. It's even easier to make than a crumble; simply fold oats into melted butter and syrup and you're there.

# apricot and blueberry oat bars

⅔ cup (1¼ sticks) unsalted butter

½ cup golden syrup (if unavailable, use corn syrup)

½ teaspoon sea salt (or kosher salt)

2 cups old-fashioned oats

8 ripe apricots

1½ cups blueberries

2 tablespoons light brown sugar

**Serves 6**

Preheat the oven to 400°F.

Gently melt the butter in a small pan with the syrup and the salt, then fold in the oats.

Quarter the apricots, removing the pits, and arrange with the blueberries in the bottom of a 12-inch (2-quart) oval gratin or other shallow ovenproof dish. Sprinkle with the sugar, and then scatter the oat bar mixture over them. There should still be some fruit showing through. Bake for 30 minutes until the top is golden and crusty. Serve about 10 minutes out of the oven. It's also delicious cold.

Pistachios and sour cherries are the wild cards here, in a crumble that goes from cookie-crisp on the very top, steadily giving up the fight as you travel down to where it meets the fruit, where it soaks up the pear juices.

# pear and sour cherry crumble

### Fruit

2 pounds pears, peeled, quartered,
cored, and thinly sliced

1 tablespoon lemon juice

¼ cup demerara sugar (raw sugar)—
or use regular sugar

½ cup dried sour cherries

### Crumble

1½ cups all-purpose flour

2 cups old-fashioned oats

1 cup demerara (raw) sugar or
regular sugar

¾ cup plus 2 tablespoons (1¾ sticks)
unsalted butter, chilled and diced

½ cup shelled pistachios

Crème fraîche or heavy cream,
for serving

### Serves 6–8

Preheat the oven to 375°F. Toss the pears in a large bowl with the lemon juice and sugar, then gently mix in the sour cherries. Arrange the fruit in a shallow 12-inch (2-quart) oval gratin or ovenproof dish.

Combine the flour, oats, sugar, and butter in a food processor, and whizz until the mixture resembles large crumbs, taking care to stop the motor before it turns into a dough. Transfer the crumble to a bowl, then mix in the nuts. Scatter the mixture over the fruit, don't worry if you have to mound it, the crumble will sink as it cooks. Bake for 40 minutes until the top is golden and crisp. Serve the crumble 20–30 minutes out of the oven with a spoonful of crème fraîche. It's also delicious cold.

Plums are a fruit that I rarely eat raw, but would be my first choice to encounter beneath a lid of sweet buttery pastry. They relax into this richly flavored compote when you cook them, spilling out sticky juices that soak into the pie crust. And this is a particularly fine custard, that will lend itself to any of the crumbles and pies in this chapter. It doesn't have to be vanilla, a little cinnamon, ground cloves, cardamom, or splash of liqueur can be used to bring out the best in whatever fruits are starring.

# plum pie with vanilla custard

## Sweet pie dough

⅔ cup (1¼ sticks) unsalted butter, softened
¾ cup sugar
2 medium eggs
3 cups all-purpose flour, sifted
½ cup ground almonds

## Vanilla custard

1¼ cups whole milk
6 medium organic egg yolks
⅓ cup sugar
1 vanilla bean, slit and cut up
⅔ cup whipping cream

## Plums

2 pounds plums, pitted and quartered
⅔ cup light brown sugar
2 tablespoons all-purpose flour
Finely grated zest of 1 lemon
Sugar, for dusting

## Serves 6

To make the pie dough, cream the butter and sugar together in a bowl using a wooden spoon until soft and fluffy. A food processor will make light work of this. Beat in the eggs until well combined, then gradually add the flour and ground almonds and bring the dough together. Wrap it in plastic wrap and chill for at least 2 hours; it will keep for several days.

To make the custard, pour the milk into a small pan and bring to a boil. Whisk the egg yolks and sugar in a bowl, then whisk in the milk. Return this to the pan and heat gently until you have a thin pouring custard that coats the back of the spoon, taking care not to overheat it. Pour it immediately into a bowl, add the vanilla bean, cover the surface with plastic wrap and let it cool. Blend the custard in a blender and strain it through a strainer, then whip the cream until it forms soft peaks and whisk it in. Cover and chill the custard until needed, and give it a good stir before serving.

Toss the plums with 2 tablespoons of the sugar in a bowl and leave for 30 minutes to draw out any excess juice, then drain them. Preheat the oven to 400°F. Let the dough come to room temperature for a few minutes, and then knead it until pliable. Thinly roll out two thirds of the dough on a lightly floured surface. Use this to line the bottom of a 2-quart pie dish or oval gratin dish, letting the extra hang over the sides. Don't worry if the dough tears and you end up partly pressing it into the dish.

Toss the plums with the remaining sugar, the flour, and lemon zest, and tip them into the pie dish. Roll out the remaining pie dough with any trimmings, paint the edge of the dough along the rim of the dish with milk and lay the rolled pie dough on top. Press the edges together, trim the sides, then crimp the edges using your fingertips or the tip of a knife. Brush the pie crust with milk, cut several diagonal slits in the center, and dust with the sugar. Bake for about 35 minutes until the crust is golden and the plums are tender. Serve hot about 10 minutes out of the oven, or at room temperature, with the custard.

This is more cake than pie, a steaming scented sponge cake atop a fluffy mass of apples. And however unlikely it seems when you put it into the oven, don't be deterred: what appears to be an impossibly thin liquid at the start shapes up nicely into a luscious caramel that coats the sponge cake by the time the oven's done its stuff.

# apple butterscotch pie

1¼ pounds cooking apples, peeled, quartered, and sliced

## Sponge cake
1 cup all-purpose flour
1½ teaspoons baking powder
⅛ teaspoon salt
¼ cup sugar
⅓ cup unsalted butter, chilled and diced
1 medium egg
scant ½ cup milk
Finely grated zest of 1 lemon
⅓ cup currants

## Sauce
⅓ cup light brown sugar
1¾ tablespoons unsalted butter
scant ½ cup water
¼ teaspoon sea salt (or kosher salt)
juice of ½ lemon

## Serves 6

Preheat the oven to 400°F. To make the sponge cake, place the flour and sugar in a bowl, and rub in the butter; this can also be done in a food processor or mixer. Now incorporate the egg and the milk, then fold in the lemon zest and the currants. Arrange the apple in the bottom of a 12-inch (2-quart) oval gratin or other shallow ovenproof dish and smooth the sponge cake mixture on top.

To make the sauce, place the sugar, butter, water, and salt in a small pan and bring to a boil. Stir in the lemon juice, then pour this mixture over the sponge cake topping. The sauce will seem very liquid at this point, but once baked, it transforms into a rich butterscotch. Bake the "pie" for 30–35 minutes until golden on the surface and bubbling around the edges. Serve 5–10 minutes out of the oven.

Wherever school cafeteria food failed, it made up for it with those big trays of cake sprinkled with sugar concealing just a little fruit in the name of goodness underneath. I prefer this kind of dessert to a steamed sponge cake, not least because it has a lovely crusty golden surface, and, can be eaten cold as well as hot. In true comfort-dessert style it's delicious with custard or crème fraîche or cream.

# baked rhubarb sponge cake

### Fruit

1¼ pounds rhubarb, trimmed
   and cut into ¾-inch lengths
⅔ cup sugar

### Sponge cake

1 cup sugar
1 cup (2 sticks) unsalted butter, diced
1¾ cups all-purpose flour
2½ teaspoons baking powder
⅛ teaspoon salt
4 medium eggs
scant ½ cup milk
Finely grated zest of 1 lemon

### Serves 6–8

Preheat the oven to 400°F. Toss the rhubarb with the sugar in a bowl and arrange over the bottom of a 12-inch (2-quart) oval gratin dish or individual ovenproof dishes if you have them.

Reserving 2 tablespoons of the sugar, place all the sponge cake ingredients in the bowl of a food processor and cream together. Smooth this on top of the rhubarb, scatter the reserved sugar over this, and bake for 40 minutes. It's at its fluffiest and most scented served hot, but also good at room temperature.

Had you ever idly pondered on what a posh crumble is like, then this should satiate your curiosity. The crumble is that much finer, and the fruit cooks in a delectable butterscotch sauce. At the Dorchester Hotel in London, this comes with all the trimmings: ripe autumn berries, Scotch whisky ice cream, and a raspberry puree, trimmings which I wouldn't expect you to prepare any more than I'd expect you to dress up to eat this.

# the Dorchester's apple and golden raisin crumble

## Fruit and butterscotch sauce

¾ cup sugar (refined)

¼ cup (½ stick) unsalted butter

3 cooking apples, peeled, cored, diced

3 tablespoons golden raisins

3 tablespoons raisins

½ teaspoon cinnamon

## Crumble

⅓ cup light brown sugar

½ cup all-purpose flour

¾ cup ground almonds

⅓ cup (¾ stick) unsalted butter

## For serving (optional)

Scotch whisky ice cream

1 cup autumn fruit (raspberries, blueberries, blackberries)

Raspberry puree

## Serves 6

Preheat the oven to 375°F. To prepare the caramel base for the fruit, place the sugar with a scant ½ cup water in a medium-large pan (one that will fit the diced apple later) and simmer over a medium heat for 10–15 minutes until a lovely toffee gold. Give it an initial stir to help the sugar dissolve, and again as it begins to color. Now add the butter in small pieces, stirring well with each addition until incorporated; by the end you should have a thick butterscotch sauce. Add the apples and cook for 4–5 minutes. Initially the sauce will sieze up, but as you continue to heat the pan it will melt again. Stir in the golden raisins and raisins, and cinnamon, and transfer to a 12-inch (2-quart) oval gratin dish or other shallow ovenproof dish.

Place all the ingredients for the crumble in the bowl of a food processor and whizz until the mixture resembles fine crumbs. Evenly scatter this over the fruit and bake for 40 minutes until lightly golden and the fruit is bubbling through at the edges.

Serve with all the trimmings if you wish, though the crumble is delicious just as it is.

# good old-fashioned

I think it's highly unlikely that we will ever forget the traditional desserts we grew up with, regardless of trends and fashions. We might tweak them, pare them down or glam them up, even give the occasional new one the honor of becoming a tradition, but they are writ large in our memories and most of us cling tenaciously to the nostalgia they recall.

Bread and butter pudding is one of the Holy Grails of the kitchen; chefs and cooks throughout the land pride themselves on making the best one around. It has now surpassed its humble beginnings as a parsimonious guise for using up yesterday's bread, enriched with a little butter and soaked in milk, eggs, and sugar, to emerge in gloriously rich versions with a lightly set creamy custard surrounding panettone, brioche, or a country bread spread with marmalade, a whole vanilla bean in its midst. And not any old dried fruit: it has to be soaked in brandy or rum.

One needs a good rice pudding up one's sleeve, too. Ideally an ambrosial cool creamy rice that can secretly be dipped into during the early hours of the morning, and at other times of the day can be scattered with all sorts of fruits, from pomegranate seeds to passion fruit.

But perhaps the new British favorite is Sticky Toffee Pudding, a steaming sponge cake rich with dates, and an unctuous toffee sauce. As you might expect from a pudding of this popularity, there are several contenders to the throne of invention. But Francis Coulson of the Sharrow Bay Country House Hotel in Penrith, just south of the Scottish border, who called it "icky sticky toffee sponge" is the man who launched it on the nation, back in 1960. How nice to think that all those hippies had great puddings as well as rock 'n' roll and free love to get them through that punishing decade.

Its name precedes it and says it in one. It was, after all, once called "icky sticky toffee pudding" after that lovely molasses-rich sauce that smothers the date sponge.

# sticky toffee pudding

## Sponge cake

1 cup pitted dates, chopped

1 cup water

2 teaspoons baking soda

⅓ cup (¾ stick) unsalted butter, diced

⅔ cup light brown sugar

2 medium eggs

2 tablespoons golden syrup
   (if unavailable, use corn syrup)

1 teaspoon vanilla extract

1½ cups all-purpose flour, sifted

## Sauce

½ cup dark brown sugar

½ cup (1 stick) unsalted butter

⅔ cup heavy cream

Heavy cream or crème fraîche,
   for serving

## Serves 6–8

Preheat the oven to 375°F and butter a 9-inch-square cake pan.

Bring the dates and water to a boil in a small pan and simmer over a low heat for 5 minutes. Remove from the heat and stir in the baking soda, which will froth up.

Cream the butter and sugar together in a food processor, add the eggs one at a time, and then the syrup, vanilla, and flour. Transfer the mixture to a large bowl and beat in the date mixture in two goes. Pour the mixture into the prepared pan and bake for 25 minutes until the top is set and the cake is risen and shrinking from the sides.

Meanwhile make the sauce. Heat the sugar, butter, and cream together in a small pan, whisking until smooth. Smooth half the sauce over the top of the cake and cut it into squares. Offer the remaining sauce separately for those that like lots. Serve with plenty of cream.

If you're British, this really hits home, but regardless of where you're from, this pudding is for everyone who loves toast and marmalade. The custard here is made with egg yolks, fresh orange juice, cream, and sugar, and is richly flavored and lightly set, it soaks into the buttered bread. The crusts on the bread that emerge golden, glazed, and chewy are the best bit, and a coarse-textured white or rye bread will be well-rewarded. Day-old bread provides just the right texture, nothing too fresh, the aim is a crumb that can hold its custard. A salty butter isn't a bad idea either.

# marmalade bread and butter pudding

Salted butter, softened

6 thin slices day-old white
     bread, with crusts

½ cup coarse-cut marmalade

1¼ cups heavy cream

1¼ cups fresh orange juice

8 medium egg yolks

½ cup sugar

## Serves 6

Butter the slices of bread on one side and spread with marmalade. Cut them into 2 triangles and lay these in two rows of overlapping slices, marmalade-side up, along the length of a 14-inch (2½-quart) oval gratin or other shallow ovenproof dish, one that will fit into a roasting pan to make a water bath. Arrange the rows at an angle to each other so the surface is even.

Pour the cream and orange juice into a small pan and bring to a boil. Whisk the egg yolks and sugar in a small bowl, then whisk in the hot cream and orange mixture and return to the pan. Gently heat, stirring constantly with a wooden spoon, until the custard thickens enough to coat the back of it. Pour this through a strainer onto the bread, as evenly as possible. Gently press down with the spoon to coat the bread thoroughly and let it stand for 15 minutes.

Preheat the oven to 400°F. Create a water bath by placing the gratin dish in a roasting pan with warm water that comes two thirds of the way up the sides of the gratin dish. Bake for 30–35 minutes until the custard has set on top, the edges of the bread are golden and crisp, and the marmalade sticky and glazed. Serve 5–10 minutes out of the oven.

In essence this is an old-fashioned bread and butter pudding, with a wobbly egg custard that's puffy and golden. But from there we depart to panettone, which contains an artful mix of dried fruits and candied peel and so does away with the need for raisins and the like, though that's not to say that you can't play it the old-fashioned way. For a traditional bread and butter pudding, scatter ⅓ cup of golden raisins and raisins, soaked in rum if you wish, over the bottom of the dish and replace the panettone with triangles of day-old white bread.

# buttered panettone pudding

3 medium eggs

¾ cup sugar

1¾ cups heavy cream

1¾ cups milk

Softened unsalted butter, for
    spreading

10–12 x ½-inch slices panettone,
    cut as wedges from a 1-pound loaf

1 vanilla bean

⅓ cup apricot jam, warmed and
    strained (optional)

**Serves 6**

Preheat the oven to 350°F. Whisk the eggs and sugar in a bowl, then whisk in the cream and milk. Butter the panettone and arrange in overlapping slices to cover the bottom of a 14-inch (2½-quart) oval gratin or other shallow ovenproof dish, one that will fit into a roasting pan to make a water bath. The center of an oval dish may take two slices side by side; the narrow ends may only hold one. Pour the custard through a strainer over and around the panettone. Tuck the vanilla bean beneath the custard in the center.

To make the water bath, place the gratin dish in a roasting pan with cold water that comes two thirds of the way up the sides of the gratin dish. Bake for 1 hour until the custard is puffy and set and the bread golden. Brush the surface of the bread with the apricot jam; this bit is optional but it gives the pudding a lovely sticky glaze. Serve immediately. The vanilla bean can be rinsed and used again.

A cooling ambrosial creamed rice to dish up with whatever fruits are in season; my choice would be pomegranate seeds in the depths of winter and some slivers of peach in summer. The more vanilla you can afford the better: one bean is a treat and two a joy, the rice should be liberally flecked with minute black seeds. And I favor risotto (arborio) rice over pudding rice—it's much better at retaining its texture and shape. Arborio and pudding rice are both types of short-grain rice and belong to the Japonica family that includes sticky rice and sushi rice; the starch of short-grain rice is altogether different from that found in basmati and other types of long-grain rice. Of the various rices used for making risottos, arborio does an excellent job, as it does here as well.

# vanilla creamed rice

## Rice

¾ cup risotto (arborio) rice

1¾ cups whole milk

1¾ tablespoons unsalted butter

¼ cup sugar

1 vanilla bean

## Custard

2 medium egg yolks

⅓ cup sugar

scant cup whole milk

⅔ cup crème fraîche (if unavailable, use heavy cream)

Seeds from 1 pomegranate, for serving

## Serves 6

Preheat the oven to 425°F. Bring a medium ovenproof pan of water to a boil, add the rice, and boil for 5 minutes, then drain.

Place the milk, butter, and sugar for the rice in the same pan and bring to a boil. Add the vanilla bean and stir in the drained rice. Return the milk to a simmer, cover the rice with a circle of baking parchment or a used butter wrapper, and then the lid. Place the pan in the oven, lower the temperature to 325°F, and cook for about 40 minutes until the rice has absorbed all the milk. Remove the pan from the oven, take out and reserve the vanilla bean, and let the rice cool.

While the rice is cooking, make the custard. Whisk together the egg yolks and sugar until pale. Bring the milk to a boil in a small pan, beat it into the egg mixture, then pour it back into the pan and cook over a very low heat until the mixture thickens and coats the back of a spoon, without allowing it to boil. Strain the custard through a strainer into a bowl or measuring cup. Open out the reserved vanilla bean and run a small sharp knife down its length to scrape out the seeds. Stir these into the custard, cover the surface with plastic wrap and let cool.

Combine the cooled rice with the custard and stir in the crème fraîche. Cover and chill for several hours or overnight. The rice is nicest eaten 30 minutes out of the fridge. Serve a mound of rice with the pomegranate seeds spooned over it.

So named because of the surprise that lies below the souffléd top, though I have slightly deviated from the original here, baking it in a water bath which creates a lovely lightly set custard below as opposed to a sauce. Some runny cream is welcome.

# lemon surprise pudding

½ cup (1 stick) unsalted butter, diced

¾ cup sugar

Zest and juice of 2 lemons

4 medium eggs, separated

3 tablespoons all-purpose flour

2 cups milk

### Serves 6

Preheat the oven to 375°F. Place the butter, sugar, and lemon zest in the bowl of a food processor and cream together until light and fluffy. Incorporate the egg yolks one by one, and then the lemon juice and the flour. Add the milk, with the motor running.

Transfer the mixture to a large bowl. Beat the egg whites until they are stiff; I use a hand-held electric beater, and fold or whisk them in two goes into the lemon mixture. Pour this into a buttered 12-inch (2-quart) oval gratin or other shallow ovenproof dish, at least 2 inches deep. Place this inside a roasting pan with warm water that comes two thirds of the way up the sides of the gratin dish and bake for 40–45 minutes until golden and risen like a soufflé. Serve immediately.

Clafoutis Limousin is one of the few puddings in the true sense of the word that the French go in for—juicy black cherries baked in a surround of sweetened batter. It can be made with all sorts of fruits, but prunes that have been slowly simmered in rum are a particular treat. It's yummiest eaten hot or lukewarm, about 30 minutes out of the oven, and I'm happy with a slice eaten in the hand with a napkin, but there are no rules against bowls and pitchers of cream either.

# prune clafoutis

## Batter

½ cup all-purpose flour, sifted

¼ cup granulated or vanilla sugar, plus extra for dusting the dish

3 medium eggs

1¾ cups milk

1¾ tablespoons unsalted butter, plus extra for greasing the dish

## Prunes

⅔ cup dark rum, plus 1 tablespoon

⅔ cup water

¼ cup granulated or vanilla sugar

7 ounces prunes, ready-soaked and pitted (about 1½ cups)

Confectioners' sugar, for dusting

## Serves 4–6

First make the batter as it needs time to rest. Put the flour, sugar, eggs, and milk in a blender and blend them until smooth and creamy. Set aside for 30 minutes. If making the batter by hand, you will probably need to give it a whisk at the end.

Put the ⅔ cup of rum, the water, and sugar for the prunes in a small pan and bring to a boil. Add the prunes and simmer for 15–25 minutes until all the liquid has been absorbed and they are coated in a sticky syrup.

Preheat the oven to 425°F. Butter a 14-inch (2½-quart) gratin dish and dust with granulated or vanilla sugar, tipping out the excess. Pour in the batter, then scatter the prunes and syrup evenly over the surface. Dot with the butter and bake for 25–30 minutes. When it comes out of the oven it will be impressively puffed and golden, sinking after a few minutes. Sprinkle the remaining tablespoon of rum over it. Dust with confectioners' sugar just before serving.

## vanilla sugar

To make vanilla sugar, cut up a vanilla bean and whizz with 1 cup sugar in a food processor, then sift it. Store in a jar and use as needed.

Seriously indulgent: the calorie-conscious should switch off now. This comes with a fluffy suet crust and a lavish pool of brown sugar and butter sauce scented with lemon inside. Only the hardy need eat the "frog"—the lemon—the crust and sauce are the best bits, but be sure to scrape out the lemon flesh from the skin.

# sussex pond pudding

Combine the flour, breadcrumbs, lemon zest, suet, and salt in a large bowl, and add just enough milk to bring the dough together. Set aside about a quarter of the dough for the lid, and roll the rest into a 10-inch circle on a lightly floured counter, and use it to line a 1-quart steamed pudding mold, folding over any pleats and pressing them into the side. Trim the top. Place half the butter and sugar in the bottom of the pudding mold. Roll the lemon on the counter and prick it all over with a skewer, nestle it on top of the butter and sugar, then place the remaining butter and sugar around the sides. Roll out the rest of the dough along with any trimmings, brush the rim of the dough in the bowl with milk, and place the lid on top, pressing the edges together to seal them, then trim the edge. Don't worry if there appears to be a little space below the lid, the sides will swell as it cooks.

Place a circle of baking parchment over the mold and tie it in position using string. Place the pudding mold in a pan with boiling water that comes halfway up the sides, cover, and cook over a low heat for 2½ hours, replenishing the water as necessary.

Remove the baking parchment, run a knife around the inside edge of the pudding, place a deep plate on top, and invert it. Serve in wedges with the buttery sauce that spills out.

scant cup all-purpose flour, sifted
1½ teaspoons baking powder
2 cups fresh white breadcrumbs
finely grated zest of 1 lemon, plus
    1 whole lemon (stalk removed)
1 cup shredded suet
Pinch of sea salt or kosher salt
About ⅓ cup milk
½ cup (1 stick) unsalted butter, diced
½ cup light brown sugar

## Serves 4–6

I love the way recipes evolve with the person who cooks them, and this is a friend Val Archer's take on Karen Perry's Danish apple cake. Not conventionally baked, alternate layers of crisp breadcrumbs are layered with an apple compote, before being chilled. And it is one of the most soothing desserts I have had, not too sweet or rich.

# brown sugar apple cake

## Puree

3⅓ pounds cooking apples, peeled, cored, and sliced

Finely grated zest of 1 lemon, and juice of ½ lemon

⅓ cup demerara (raw) sugar (or regular sugar)

½ cup golden raisins

3 cloves

1 teaspoon vanilla extract

## Crumb layer

½ cup (1 stick) unsalted butter

10 ounces dry white breadcrumbs (about 3½ cups)

¾ cup ground almonds

⅔ cup sugar

Few drops of almond extract

⅓ cup toasted almonds (see page 97)

Confectioners' sugar for dusting

Whipped cream or vanilla ice cream, for serving (optional)

## Makes 1 x 8-inch cake
## Serves 6–8

Place the apples in a large pan with the lemon zest and juice and add just enough water to prevent the fruit from sticking to the bottom, only to a depth of ⅛ inch or so. Add the sugar, raisins, cloves, and vanilla, bring to a boil, then cover and cook over a low heat for 10–20 minutes until soft, stirring halfway through. If the apples are sitting in a lot of juice, simmer to reduce it. You should end up with a chunky puree. Discard the cloves.

You need to cook the crumbs in two goes. Melt half the butter in a large frying pan over a medium heat, add half the breadcrumbs and half the ground almonds and fry, stirring almost constantly until lightly golden and crisp. Add half the sugar once the crumbs begin to color. Transfer to a bowl and cook the remaining half of the ingredients in the same way. Stir in a few drops of almond extract.

Scatter a quarter of the breadcrumb mixture over the bottom of an 8-inch cake pan that's at least 1½ inches deep and has a removable bottom. Spread a third of the apple puree on top, then two more alternating layers of crumbs and apples, finishing with crumbs. Chill uncovered for 6–8 hours, or overnight.

To serve, run a knife around the inside edge of the pan and unclip and remove the collar. Scatter the toasted almonds over the cake and dust with confectioners' sugar. Accompany with whipped cream or vanilla ice cream if you wish. It is at its best chilled, and eaten within a day while the crumbs on top are still crisp, though it will be tasty for several days afterwards.

Strains of British summer pudding here, bread toasted to a buttery crisp in the oven, soaking up the juices of a warm berry compote. A spoonful of clotted cream hovers as an idea above it.

# berry charlotte

1¾ pounds mixture of raspberries
   and blackberries (about 5½–6 cups)
2 cups redcurrants
1 tablespooon flour
¾ cup sugar
6 thin slices white bread
Softened unsalted butter, for spreading

Serves 6

Preheat the oven to 400°F. Combine the berries and currants in a large bowl, sprinkle the flour and sugar over them, and toss to combine. Tip the mixture into a 12 x 8-inch baking dish.

Cut off the crusts from the bread, squaring the slices. Butter them on both sides and cut each slice into 4 triangles. Lay these in three overlapping rows on top of the fruit and bake for 30–35 minutes until the bread is golden and crisp on the surface and the fruit is bubbling. Let it stand for 10 minutes before serving.

To me, this one has the appearance of the kind of luscious dessert that you might offer up had you been a farmer's wife in America's Midwest during the time of the California Gold Rush, and I couldn't resist including it. It lies somewhere in between a cheesecake and a sponge cake, set with big juicy red cherries.

# cherry cheesecake cake

## Batter

5 tablespoons white wine

¾ cup sugar

¼ teaspoon baking soda

2 medium eggs

¼ cup peanut oil

1 teaspoon vanilla extract

⅔ cup all-purpose flour, sifted

1½ teaspoons baking powder

⅛ teaspoon salt

## Topping

1 cup sour cream

⅓ cup confectioners' sugar

¾ cup cherries, pitted

## Makes 1 x 8-inch cake
## Serves 6–8

Preheat the oven to 350°F and lightly oil the inside of an 8-inch cake pan, one at least 2 inches deep, and with a removable bottom.

Heat the wine and half the sugar in a small pan over a lowish heat, stirring until the sugar melts, then stir in the baking soda and set aside for about 20 minutes.

Whisk the remaining sugar with one of the eggs, the oil, and vanilla in a bowl, then stir in the flour, baking powder, and salt, and the wine mixture, half at a time, alternately. Transfer the cake batter to the prepared pan and bake for 25 minutes until firm and shrinking from the sides.

Increase the temperature to 400°F. Whisk the sour cream with the confectioners' sugar in a bowl, then whisk in the remaining egg. Smooth this over the surface of the cake, scatter the cherries on top, and return to the oven for about 25 minutes until the filling is golden at the edges. Let it cool, then run a knife around the inside edge of the cake pan and unclip to remove the collar, and serve.

A tart that kills on looks, from *Baking with Passion* by Dan Lepard and Richard Whittington—recipes from the wonderful patisserie in London, Baker and Spice: it tastes divine, too. They do, of course, make their own puff pastry, and you don't have to, but do try to find one made with butter and not vegetable fat—check out the freezer section.

# plum and frangipane tart

8 ounces puff pastry dough

9 slightly under-ripe Victoria plums (or other small, sweet plums), quartered and pitted

3 tablespoons apricot jam, warmed and strained

## Frangipane

¾ cup plus 2 tablespoons (1¾ sticks) softened unsalted butter

¾ cup sugar

1¼ cups ground almonds

1¼ cups ground hazelnuts*

¾ cup flour

3 medium eggs

## Makes 1 x 10-inch tart
## Serves 6–8

Preheat the oven to 400°F. Make the frangipane first. Blend the butter with the sugar in a food processor for about 8 minutes. Add the ground nuts and flour and beat briefly, then whisk in the eggs, one at a time. Set the frangipane aside.

Roll out the dough into a thin circle on a lightly floured surface, and cut out a circle to fit a 10-inch tart pan. Use the rolling pin to gently lift the dough into the pan and press it into the bottom and the sides. Roll the rolling pin across the top to trim the edges.

Spread the frangipane over the pie crust, and arrange the plum quarters cut-side up on top, laying them in circles starting at the outside. Bake for 15 minutes, then reduce the temperature to 325°F and bake for another 35–45 minutes by which time the frangipane will have risen up around the plums and set. Brush the surface of the tart with the warmed jam and let it cool.

* While you can buy ready-ground almonds, you may need to grind your own hazelnuts in an electric coffee grinder. Alternatively substitute ground almonds.

Crema Catalana is the Spanish equivalent of crème brûlée, every bit as silky and sinful, here served as a tart filling on a buttery cookie crust.

# custard tart

## Custard

3 gelatin leaves, cut into broad
  strips (or 1 envelope granulated
  gelatin, see page 47)
2½ cups light cream
⅔ cup sugar
1 cinnamon stick
2 strips lemon zest
6 medium organic egg yolks
Confectioners' sugar, for dusting

## Almond Crust

1¼ cups slivered almonds, toasted
  (see page 97)
6 ounces sweet buttery cookies
  (e.g., shortbread) (to yield
  3–3½ cups crumbs)
3 tablespoons unsalted butter

## Makes 1 x 8-inch tart
## Serves 6–8

Place the gelatin strips in a bowl, cover with cold water, and soak for 5 minutes, then drain. Put the cream, sugar, cinnamon, and lemon zest in a small nonstick pan and bring almost to a boil, stirring occasionally so the sugar melts. Put the yolks in a bowl and whisk the cream mixture into them, it will thicken instantly into a thin custard. Pour a little over the gelatin, stir to dissolve, then add it back to the rest of the custard. Strain through a strainer, then cover and let cool, and chill for 3–4 hours until semi-set.

Meanwhile, preheat the oven to 400°F. Briefly whizz half the toasted almonds in a food processor to coarsely chop, then remove. Break up the cookies and whizz to crumbs, again in the food processor. Gently melt the butter in a small pan over a low heat, tip in the crumbs and chopped almonds, and stir to coat them. Press the mixture into the bottom of an 8-inch cake pan, one that's 3½ inches deep and with a removable bottom. Chill it.

Spoon the semi-set custard over the crust, smoothing the surface with the back of a spoon, then cover and chill overnight. Remove from the fridge 15 minutes before serving. Scatter the remaining almonds over the top and liberally dust with confectioners' sugar. Run a knife around the inside edge of the pan and unclip and remove the collar. Serve in slices.

A British summer pudding consists of a shell of white bread slices soaked in dramatically dark, sultry crimson juices encasing a compote: unlikely but true. It may have been invented as a healthy alternative to richer 18th-century offerings, though not with a spoonful of clotted cream. For a connoisseur's pudding, it's surprising how rarely you come across a really good one. While it's not difficult to get right, it's easy to get it wrong. The bread should be a loaf of day-old white bread and the slices must be used to line the glass bowl as seamlessly as possible—any cracks will allow the juice to seep out once the pudding has been inverted.

# summer pudding

2 cups red currants

2 cups black currants

¾ cup sugar

1½ pounds raspberries, blackberries, or loganberries (about 4½–5½ cups)

¾ unsliced loaf of day-old white bread, sliced by hand about 5⁄16-inch thick (you need 8–10 slices)

Clotted cream (or heavy cream, if unavailable), for serving

Serves 6

To "string the currants," slide a fork into the stalk and pass the stalk through the fork tines to release the currants. Put the currants and sugar in a small pan, heat 4–5 minutes until the fruit is soft but still retains its shape, and is sitting in a pool of syrup. Place half the currants in a strainer and press the juice into a bowl and then return it to the pan, discarding the solids. Fold in the other berries, stir well, and heat very gently for a minute or two, not to cook them but to encourage them to release their juices. Let the fruit cool, then adjust the sweetness if necessary with a little more sugar. Set aside about two thirds of a teacup of the fruit and juice, cover and put in the fridge.

Remove the crusts from the bread and line a deep 2-quart glass bowl. Place a square of bread on the bottom of the bowl with four pieces around the sides, and fill in the triangular gaps as neatly as possible. Tip the fruit into the bowl and press it down well using a wooden spoon. Make a lid with more bread, and trim the tops of the sides level with the lid. Place a small plate over the top, slightly smaller than the width of the bowl, and put a weight on top (unopened cans are ideal). Leave the pudding in the fridge overnight.

To serve, run a knife carefully around the inside edge of the bowl to loosen it, and then invert the pudding onto a plate. Let the pudding stand for 30–60 minutes, which will bring it back up to room temperature and will also let the juices soak into the bottom. Spoon the reserved fruit and juices over the top, soaking any bits of bread that haven't turned red. Serve it with plenty of clotted cream.

festive

Christmas, Thanksgiving, and Easter are times when we throw off our shackles and call up all the good things in life. We can relax and linger at the table, eat a little bit more and drink a little bit more, and stop rushing. The chances are there will be plenty of takers for any desserts, festive or otherwise, which is good news for the cook as they rarely come in half sizes and you want lots of eager diners to do them justice.

There are scents and flavors that we hope and expect to find at these times of year, ones that we associate with our childhood, which immediately bring the memories flooding back. At Christmas it's a mass of dried fruits and candied peel, warming spices such as cinnamon, a grating of nutmeg, a hint of cloves, and the warming rasp of brandy and rum. Whether they're woven into a plum pudding or a mincemeat pie, they are as evocative as the scent of pine needles and wood smoke.

At Easter, we play with the same spices, a lighter touch with the fruit and candied peel perhaps, and more in the way of color. We may not have the same traditional greats at this time of year, but a bread and butter pudding made with hot cross buns, a creamy charlotte with a cassata-like heart, or a bakewell tart all seem to herald primroses and violets in the banks and blackthorn in blossom in the hedgerows, picked out by a clear blue sky. And, of course, chocolate in any guise will be wolfed down, regardless of all those eggs on the sideboard.

Both the roulade and the remaining cranberry puree can be frozen ahead of time, which helps your advance Christmas planning. Wrap the roulade in the paper, pop it inside a large freezer bag, and freeze. Given its delicacy, I prefer to remove the paper first and leave it loosely covered with plastic on a plate to thaw for a couple of hours before serving.

# cranberry ripple roulade

18 ounces cranberries (about 5 cups)
1¾ cups sugar (refined)
Confectioners' sugar, for dusting
5 medium egg whites, at room temperature
1¼ cups whipping cream

### Serves 6–8

Place the cranberries in a medium pan with ½ cup of the sugar, cover, and cook over a medium-low heat for 10–15 minutes, stirring halfway through, until the berries are soft and surrounded by juice. Press the cranberries and juice through a strainer, then return the puree to the pan and simmer to reduce it by about half, stirring towards the end. Pour it into a bowl, cover, and let cool, then chill it for about an hour before you start the roulade.

Preheat the oven to 400°F. Butter and line a 12 x 8-inch jelly roll pan with baking parchment (or foil). Cut out a sheet of the parchment (or foil), 16 x 12 inches, and dust lightly with confectioners' sugar and set aside. Beat the egg whites in a large bowl until stiff, then sprinkle a tablespoon at a time of the remaining sugar over them, beating well with each addition, until you have a stiff, glossy meringue; I use a hand-held electric beater. Spoon it into the pan, and level it. Place in the oven, reduce the heat to 325°F and bake for 15 minutes until lightly golden and firm when pressed.

Run a knife around the edge of the meringue and turn out onto the large sheet of parchment (or foil). Let cool to room temperature for 15–20 minutes. Whip the cream until it forms fluffy but firm peaks. Stir the cranberry puree to thin it, then spoon a third of it over the surface of the cream and fold it over a couple of times to marble it. Remove the top paper from the meringue, spoon the cream down the center, and smooth it over the top using a pastry spatula, leaving a rim. Now roll the roulade up, from a short end, using the parchment or foil underneath to help. Place on a plate and chill until needed. Liberally dust with confectioners' sugar shortly before eating, and serve in slices with the remaining puree drizzled over it.

Still dreaming of white Christmases? This snow-clad mountain, a close relation to a *bûche de noël*, conceals a heart of chocolate chestnut cream. For the full Christmas schmaltz, you could adorn the sides with little trees and skiers.

# snowy mountain

## Center

3½ ounces dark chocolate
   (about 70% cocoa), broken up
   (about ½–⅔ cup)
3½ tablespoons unsalted butter, diced
1 x 15-ounce can unsweetened
   chestnut puree
⅓ cup sugar
⅓ cup heavy cream
1 teaspoon vanilla extract

## Frosting

1 medium egg
½ cup confectioners' sugar, sifted
3 tablespoons all-purpose flour, sifted
⅔ cup whole milk
½ teaspoon vanilla extract
⅓ cup (¾ stick) unsalted butter, softened

## For decoration

Grated white chocolate
Confectioners' sugar, for dusting

## Serves 6–8

Place the chocolate and butter in the top of a double boiler over simmering water and gently melt, stirring now and again until smooth and amalgamated. Set aside to cool: the chocolate needs to be at room temperature for the next stage.

Place the chestnut puree, sugar, cream, and vanilla in the bowl of a food processor and whizz until creamy. Add the cooled chocolate and whizz again until you have a silky puree the consistency of whipped butter icing–firm enough to shape. If it seems a little loose, transfer the mixture to a bowl, cover, and chill until it firms up.

Pile the mixture in the middle of a plate or cake board at least 8 inches across and shape into a cone. Put in the fridge to set for several hours, or overnight– in which case cover it after a few hours. To make the frosting, whisk the egg and confectioners' sugar in a small nonstick pan until smooth, then whisk in the flour. Bring the milk to a boil in a small pan, and whisk it into the egg mixture. Cook the mixture over a low heat for a few minutes until the custard thickens, stirring vigorously with a wooden spoon to disperse any lumps. The custard shouldn't boil, but the odd bubble shows it's hot enough to thicken properly. Cook it for a few minutes longer, stirring constantly. Strain the custard through a strainer into a bowl, stir in the vanilla, cover the surface with plastic wrap and let cool completely.

Beat the softened butter until light and creamy. Gradually whisk in the cooled custard; I use a hand-held electric beater, then whisk for a few minutes, initially on low and then on a higher speed, until white and fluffy. Using a pastry spatula, smooth this over the chocolate cone. Pile grated chocolate on the crest to resemble newly fallen snow, and dust with confectioners' sugar. Loosely cover with plastic wrap and chill for a few hours. It keeps well for several days. I like to serve it about 30 minutes out of the fridge.

# last-minute christmas pudding (plum pudding)

I took great encouragement the first Christmas I dished this one up to my family from the fact that my mum, who has always made her Christmas puddings months in advance, gave it the thumbs up over a traditional matured pudding. Perhaps that's because it's lighter than the norm, and seems to slip down more easily.

You can make it ahead of the main course, and leave it standing in the pan. Equally though you can cook it a day or two ahead (or freeze and defrost it), and steam it for an hour to reheat. In this case, remove the paper once it is cooked, cover it with plastic wrap, and put fresh paper on before rewarming. Whisk 1–2 tablespoons dark rum and ⅓–½ cup sifted confectioners' sugar into a cup or so of crème fraîche (or heavy cream) to make a boozy cream, or simply serve it plain.

¾ cup raisins

¾ cup golden raisins

1½ cups currants

scant ½ cup stout (e.g., Guinness)

4 tablespoons brandy

¾ cup finely chopped candied peel
   (citrons)

½ cup finely chopped blanched
   almonds

½ cup undyed candied cherries,
   coarsely chopped

½ teaspoon each ground cinnamon
   and nutmeg

½ cup plus 1 tablespoon (1⅛ sticks)
   unsalted butter

⅔ cup dark brown sugar

2 medium eggs

1 tablespoon treacle (or molasses)

1¼ cups all-purpose flour, sifted

1½ tablespoons baking powder

⅛ teaspoon salt

3½ tablespoons milk

## For serving

Rum cream (see introduction,
   opposite) or crème fraîche

## Serves 6–8

Place the dried fruits in a small pan with the stout and brandy and gently simmer, stirring occasionally, until all the liquor has been absorbed. Transfer the fruit to a large mixing bowl and let it cool for 20–30 minutes. Stir in the peel, almonds, cherries, and spices.

Cream the butter and sugar together for several minutes in a food processor, then incorporate the eggs, one by one, then the treacle, the remaining dry ingredients, and finally the milk. Blend the cake mixture with the dried fruit mixture.

Butter a 5-cup (40-oz) pudding mold, line the bottom with baking parchment and butter this also. Spoon the mixture into the pudding mold and smooth the surface. Cut out two circles of baking parchment to cover the surface of the pudding, with several inches to spare on either side. Lay them on top of each other, pleated in the center, butter the surface that will come into contact with the pudding, and place over the top. Tightly tie the paper in place with string, just below the rim of the pudding mold. Place in a large pan with boiling water that comes two-thirds of the way up the sides of the pudding mold, to make a stovetop water bath, and cover and simmer over a low heat for 2½ hours. Check the water level now and again and top it up if necessary.

Run a knife around the inside rim of the pudding mold and invert onto a plate. Serve with the cream.

Baked Alaska has always spelled a grand finale, of the same era as crêpes suzettes and all things flambéed. But here the snowy mountain of warm marshmallow-like meringue conceals Christmas pudding, and cooling ice cream just beginning to melt. You might pop a little holly in the top, too.

# christmas pudding alaska

1 x 1-pint tub of vanilla
  (or other spice-flavored) ice cream
1 x 1-pound Christmas pudding
4 medium egg whites
1 cup sugar

### Serves 6

The trick is to have everything ready for the pudding in plenty of time for dinner, so that it can be quickly assembled just before serving. Several hours before eating, remove the ice cream from the freezer and let it soften for 20 minutes. Then slice it across ½-inch thick, and lay the slices out on a small baking tray or a jelly roll pan that will fit into the freezer. Loosely cover the ice cream with plastic wrap and return to the freezer to harden.

About an hour before eating, prepare the stovetop water bath: place the pudding mold with the Christmas pudding in it into a saucepan with water that comes a third of the way up the sides of the pudding mold. Bring to a boil, then cover and simmer over a low heat for 1 hour. Remove from the heat and leave the pudding in the pan while you eat your main course.

The raw meringue will hold for up to 60 minutes, so you can either whisk it before you eat, or just before dessert. Preheat the oven to 475°F. Beat the egg whites in a large bowl until stiff. Gradually sprinkle the sugar over them, beating between each addition until you have a stiff and glossy meringue.

Turn out the hot Christmas pudding onto a board and slice it into about 8 wedges. Arrange these in two rows side by side on a baking tray (lined with foil if you like), so the slices overlap like roof tiles. Ease the ice cream slices off the baking sheet using a spatula and lay them on top, again in two rows. Smooth the meringue over the sides and top so the Christmas pudding and ice cream are completely concealed. Bake for 3–4 minutes until the meringue is set and turning a pale gold. Serve immediately from the baking tray.

This has a relaxed, rustic feel to it, a big slab of tart that can be cut any size you want, and there's no rolling out of pie dough, which may find fans among you at the busy time of Christmas. The lemon and the apples cut through the sweetness of the mincemeat, and walnuts too are something in the way of distraction.

# apple, walnut, and mincemeat tart

### Walnut Pie Crust

¾ cup (1½ sticks) unsalted butter, diced
⅓ cup sugar
1 cup plus 2 tablespoons all-purpose flour
1 teaspoon baking powder, sifted
1 cup walnut pieces
2 medium egg yolks

### Mincemeat Top

Finely grated zest of 1 lemon
14 ounces mincemeat (about 1¾ cups)
3 eating apples, peeled, cored, and finely sliced into rings
3½ tablespoons unsalted butter
3 teaspoons sugar
3 tablespoons apricot jam

### Makes 12 slices

Preheat the oven to 400°F and butter a 12 x 9 x 1½-inch baking pan.

To make the walnut crust, whizz the butter, sugar, flour, baking powder, and walnuts in a food processor until the mixture starts to cling together, then add the egg yolks and continue to process to a sticky dough. Press this into the bottom of the cake pan, laying a sheet of plastic wrap or waxed paper over the top and smoothing it with your fingers, then remove it. Bake for 15–20 minutes until lightly golden and slightly risen.

Stir the lemon zest into the mincemeat in a bowl, then smooth it over the walnut crust as evenly as possible; you may have small gaps here and there depending on the texture of the mincemeat. Lay the apple slices lengthwise in three overlapping rows, discarding the bottom slice, then dot with the butter and scatter the sugar over it. Bake for 20–25 minutes until the edges of the apple slices have begun to color. Remove from the oven and run a knife around the edge of the tart, then letting it cool completely. Gently warm the jam, press it through a strainer, and lightly brush the apple slices to glaze them, then let it set.

Cut the tart into about 12 squares using a bread knife. You can either store the tart in the pan, covering it with plastic wrap, or transfer the slices to an airtight container. They should keep well for several days.

Hot cross buns are full of dried fruit and spices and by Easter Monday, when you've had your fill of them for breakfast, they should be the perfect "day-old" consistency for this classic old-fashioned bread and butter pudding.

# hot cross bun pudding

3 medium eggs
¾ cup sugar
1¾ cups heavy cream
1¾ cups milk
Salted butter, for spreading

About 5-6 hot cross buns,
   sliced into 3 discs
1 vanilla bean
⅓ cup apricot jam, warmed and
   strained (optional)

**Serves 6**

Preheat the oven to 350°F. Whisk the eggs and sugar in a bowl, then whisk in the cream and milk. Select a 14-inch (about 2½-quart) oval gratin or other shallow ovenproof dish, that fits inside a roasting pan for a water bath. Butter the hot cross bun slices, including the cross, and arrange, buttered-side up, fitting them into the dish as compactly as possible. Pour the custard through a strainer over and around the buns, and submerge the vanilla bean in the custard in the center.

Place the gratin dish in the roasting pan with enough cold water in it so that it comes two thirds of the way up the sides of the gratin dish. Bake for 1 hour until the custard is puffy and set and the bread golden. Brush the surface of the bread with the apricot jam, this bit is optional but it gives the pudding a lovely sticky glaze. Serve immediately. The vanilla bean can be rinsed and used again.

This one spans festivities, it's great at Christmas as well as at Easter, and like all the best tarts, you can serve it for elevens, afternoon tea, or for dessert with a spoonful of crème fraîche or other cream.

# marzipan bakewell

## Pastry dough

¼ cup (½ stick) unsalted butter, softened

⅓ cup sugar

½ medium egg

scant cup all-purpose flour, sifted

2½ tablespoons ground almonds

## Filling

4½ ounces ready-made marzipan
   (a heaping ⅓ cup)

3½ tablespoons unsalted butter, diced

⅓ cup sugar

2 medium eggs

1 heaping cup ground almonds

½ teaspoon baking powder, sifted

⅓ cup raisins

⅓ cup raspberry jam

⅓ cup slivered almonds

Confectioners' sugar, for dusting

## Serves 6–8

To make the pastry dough, cream the butter and sugar together in a food processor. Mix in the egg, then add the flour and ground almonds. As soon as the dough begins to form a ball, wrap it in plastic wrap and chill for at least 2 hours; it can be kept in the fridge for several days.

Preheat the oven to 375°F. Thinly roll out the dough on a lightly floured surface and line the bottom and sides of a 9 x 1¼-inch removable-bottomed fluted tart pan, trimming the excess. Don't worry if it tears and you end up partly pressing it into the pan. Line the pie crust with foil and weight it with baking beans or dried beans. Cook for 15–20 minutes until lightly colored, then remove the foil and beans.

Meanwhile, thinly roll out the marzipan on a lightly floured surface, and cut out a 9-inch circle. Cream the butter and sugar together in a food processor, then add the eggs, one at a time, the ground almonds, and baking powder. With the motor off, stir in the raisins. Lay the circle of marizpan over the pie crust, spread with the raspberry jam, then spoon the almond batter on top, smoothing the surface. Scatter the slivered almonds over it and return to the oven for 25–30 minutes until golden and risen. The tart is delicious eaten 20–30 minutes out of the oven, otherwise let it cool, then dust with confectioners' sugar. The tart keeps well for several days in an airtight container.

A crisp shell with a gooey dark chocolate meringue inside, whipped cream streaked with chocolate on top, and a few sugar-coated mini eggs for decoration. As lavish as it sounds.

# chocolate pavlova

## Pavlova

6 large egg whites, at room temperature

1¾ cups superfine sugar

1 tablespoon cornstarch, sifted

5 tablespoons cocoa powder, sifted

1 teaspoon white wine vinegar

## Top

3½ ounces milk chocolate, broken
  into pieces (about ½–⅓ cup)

1¼ cups whipping cream, whipped

Sugar-coated mini eggs for decoration

## Serves 6

Preheat the oven to 425°F. Using a hand-held electric beater, beat the egg whites in a bowl until they form stiff peaks, then scatter over it, a few tablespoons at a time, the sugar, beating well with each addition. Gradually beat in the cornstarch and cocoa, and then the vinegar, by which time you should have a very stiff, glossy meringue.

Cut out a circle of baking parchment (or foil) about 9 inches in diameter, and place this on a baking sheet. Spoon the mixture onto the circle, taking it almost to the edge of the paper, and swirl the top with the spoon. Place the pavlova in the oven, reduce the temperature to its very lowest setting (about 250°F) and bake for 1½ hours. Remove the pavlova from the oven, and let it cool. This needs to be made on the day it is to be eaten.

Gently melt the chocolate in the top of a double boiler over a little simmering water, then let it cool to room temperature. Carefully tip the meringue onto its side, gently pull off the paper, and place the pavlova on a large serving plate. Drizzle the chocolate over the whipped cream, and fold over a couple of times until it appears marbled. Spoon the cream into the center of the pavlova. You can prepare it to this point up to an hour in advance, in which case chill it.

Pile some little eggs into the center shortly before serving.

An Easter bonnet special, you could almost wear this one, with a center something like an Italian cassata.

# easter charlotte

Finely grated zest of 1 lemon,
  plus the juice, strained
⅓ cup sugar
⅓ cup water
4 gelatin leaves, cut into broad strips
  (or 1½ envelopes granulated gelatin,
  see page 47)
⅔ cup heavy cream
5 ounces ladyfingers
1 pound, 10 ounces ricotta (about
  3¼ cups), at room temperature
1¼ cups confectioners' sugar
2 tablespoons dark rum
4 medium organic egg whites
½ cup candied mixed peel (citrons)
Confectioners' sugar, for dusting
Edible paper roses or sugared violets,
  for decoration*

Serves 6

Place the lemon juice and sugar in a small pan with the water, bring to a boil, and stir until the sugar dissolves. Pour into a shallow bowl and let cool. Line the bottom of an 8-inch soufflé dish with baking parchment.

Place the gelatin strips in a bowl, cover with cold water, and soak for 5 minutes, then drain. Gently heat the cream in a small pan until it feels hot to the touch, pour it over the soaked gelatin, and stir to dissolve. Let it cool to room temperature.

Briefly dip the underside of each ladyfinger in the lemon syrup, and then use them to line the sides of the dish, standing them upright and placing them sugared-side out. Whizz the ricotta, cream, lemon zest, confectioners' sugar, and rum together in a food processor. Transfer the mixture to a large bowl. Beat the egg whites in another large bowl until stiff; I use a hand-held electric beater for this, and fold into the ricotta cream in two or three goes. Fold in the candied peel and fill the prepared soufflé dish with the mixture, smoothing the surface. Cover with plastic wrap and chill overnight.

To serve, place a plate on top of the dish and invert the pudding, then carefully peel off the paper. Dust with confectioners' sugar and decorate with edible paper roses or sugared violets.

* Jane Asher's website is a boon for decorating this kind of dessert–all sorts of edible paper and sugared flowers can be ordered from www.jane-asher.co.uk.

# index

# acknowledgements

With very many thanks to Angela Mason, Food Editor on YOU Magazine, to Sue Peart, Editor, and John Koski, Associated Editor. Also to my agent Rosemary Sandberg at Ed Victor, to Stephanie Evans, Editor, Sophie Allen, Editorial Assistant, and to Kyle Cathie.